"Have you ever gone to a foreign country where you didn't speak the language and found yourself stymied at every turn, unable to communicate even your simplest questions? Making decisions regarding real estate transactions can stop you cold if you are unfamiliar with the specialized terminology that real estate professionals use for communicating with each other, bankers, investors, courthouse personnel, and clients.

As a Realtor® and a residential property manager for more than 20 years, I found *The Complete Dictionary of Real Estate Terms* an essential tool for anyone preparing to purchase real property or to embark on a career path in real estate. The book is also a valuable resource to help real estate professionals sharpen their verbal skills as they conduct their day-to-day business. Using *The Complete Dictionary of Real Estate Terms* as a reference will certainly improve your chances for success in the real estate field and help make you a cut above those who have failed to educate themselves properly."

Karen A. Ebert, REALTOR, RMP, MPM, e-PRO
President, Austin Landmark Property Services,
Inc. ALPS, CRMC
Certified Residential Management Company
karen@alpsmgmt.com

"Even after 20 years as a real estate investor I was pleasantly surprised as the number of terms that where I did not have a good working definition. Having looked up a specific term I found myself wanting to check a few more to see what else I could learn. Definitely a reference source to keep handy when working your deals."

John B. Corey Jr.
Chelsea Private Equity LLC
12725 SW Millikan Way
Suite 300
Beaveerton OR 97005

THE

COMPLETE

DICTIONARY OF

REAL ESTATE

TERMS

EXPLAINED SIMPLY

What Smart Investors Need to Know

Jeff Haden

The Complete Dictionary of Real Estate Terms Explained Simply: What Smart Investors Need to Know

ISBN-13: 978-0910627-01-6   ISBN-10: 0-910627-01-0

Library of Congress Cataloging-in-Publication Data
Haden, Jeff (William Jeffrey), 1960-
  The complete dictionary of real estate terms explained simply : what smart investors need to know.
    p. cm.
  Includes bibliographical references and index.
  ISBN-13: 978-0-910627-01-6 (alk. paper)
  ISBN-10: 0-910627-01-0 (alk. paper)
  1. Real estate business--Dictionaries. 2. Real property--Dictionaries. 3. Real estate investment--Dictionaries. I. Title.
  HD1365.H33 2006
  333.3303--dc22
                                    2006029746

EDITOR: Marie Lujanac, mlujanac817@yahoo.com
PROOFREADER: Angela C. Adams, angela.c.adams@hotmail.com
ART DIRECTION & INTERIOR DESIGN: Meg Buchner • megadesn@mchsi.com
COVER DESIGN: Lisa Peterson, Michael Meister • info@6sense.net
BOOK PRODUCTION DESIGN: Cyanotype Book Architects • www.cyanotype.ca

For more than 20 years as a licensed real estate broker, I have enjoyed a wonderful, exciting career helping: people succeed with the largest investment of their lives and attaining the dream of home ownership; corporations with their unique needs find suitable space; investors gaining the right property for their goals; and, development of projects. Fundamental to all consumers making good decisions is an understanding of the language of Real Estate.

Real estate is a unique business that transcends time and cultures, yet the basic concepts are timeless. To enter the real estate arena at any level, one must be able to carry on a conversation with industry professionals so key decisions may be made in a timely manner and without hesitation. As is often said, "Time is of the essence".

Many people feel overwhelmed when it comes down to executing the real estate contract package or closing documents, where sometimes the papers can number in the hundreds, and an attempt to read these documents often proves disheartening, and many times professionals wonder if people sign blindly for fear of looking ignorant.

To plan for an anticipated transaction, one may ask their broker for an outline of the acquisition, disposition or lease process as well as blank copies of documents that will need to be approved and executed. Given quiet time to study, many questions will surface, as at first glance the text may prove to appear as a foreign language. One will need to research further in order to have a coherent and comprehensive understanding of exactly what they have to sign.

Today, we often hear of real estate investors making a killing in the marketplace and at the same time speculators loosing their shirts. Basically what separates "Speculators" from "Investors" is a knowledge and understanding of the unique language of real estate; how a standard dictionary defines a word does not necessarily apply in all situations. In my opinion, the main problem is, people need to decide "I am going to invest in myself and gain a thorough understanding of what I am doing to make the best decision possible, in any given situation, and in a timely manner".

The Complete Dictionary of Real Estate Terms is the perfect tool to own and keep as your ready reference containing over 2,400 real estate specific terms. Whether you are doing preliminary research in the real estate market, studying contracts and forms as you contemplate your purchase or investment, or while sitting at the closing table *The Complete Dictionary of Real Estate Terms* will prove to be a most valuable resource in your key decision-making process. Arranged in alphabetical order, each term is clearly defined in language that is easy for you to understand. You will begin to feel even more confident about your actions as you gain valuable understanding of real estate terms.

The Complete Dictionary of Real Estate Terms helps you lay a solid foundation for your success in real estate. All you need to do is apply the valuable knowledge contained in this book to build your real estate future.

I wish you happiness and great success in all your real estate dealings!

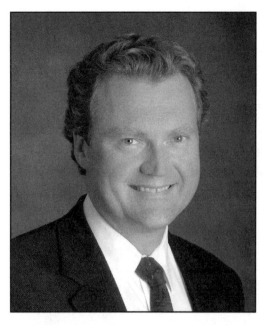

John D. Pinson
Chairman, John D.
Pinson, Inc.
CIPS, CRS, GRI, FIREC,
Cert. FIABCI
(International Real Estate
Federation)

John is an experienced licensed broker who offers "the best in real estate" in Florida, New York and Internationally. He is much sought after as a leading industry speaker and has traveled to over 40 countries meeting with government officials, addressing audiences and promoting real estate products and services. He served as 2004 Chairman, Realtors Assn. Of the Palm Beaches; 2005-06 President of FIABCI-USA; and serves on the Board of Florida Assn. of Realtors, National Assn. of Realtors, and FIABCI International, as well as several other charitable organizations.

Visit his Web site at: www.johnpinson.com, or he may be contacted at john@pinson.com.

AUTHOR

J eff Haden bought his first home while still in college; since then he's invested extensively in residential and commercial properties in five states. He has also written extensively on real estate investing, mortgages, and personal finance. A graduate of James Madison University, he is also President of BlackBird Media, an advertising agency and book publishing services provider.

Dedicated to my grandfather, who looked at the first house I wanted to buy and said, "Are you sure you shouldn't just keep your apartment?" And to my wife, who immediately looks past what is to see what could be.

I f knowledge is power, I was in trouble. I had worked my way through college, paying my way and saving enough money for a down payment on a house. I knew what I was looking for – basically any house I could afford – and I knew a little about construction, having built additions with my father as a teenager, but otherwise I knew nothing about real estate.

So I did what seemed sensible: I called a real estate agent. The next day I was riding from house to house with not one but two agents, both speaking a language I didn't understand. They casually tossed around terms like "cloud on title," "superadequacy," "trust deed," "blanket loan," "xylotomous," none of which made sense to me. I had been excited about buying a house but now it seemed very complicated and, to be honest, more than a little intimidating.

The real estate industry, just like almost any other industry, has a language all its own. Knowing that language won't automatically make you a better investor because good real estate investors have an eye for value, keep their fingers on the pulse of their market, and see the potential in properties that others can't see. But good investors also know the language of the business, and understanding real estate terms and phrases can help you make better decisions when you buy, sell, or rent a property. Plus, you'll feel more confident and assured when you interact with real estate professionals.

And if a prospective buyer of your home says, "We like your home, but what if xylotomous insects are present?" you can reply, "You're worried about wood boring insects? No problem. We'll perform a termite inspection before the closing."

— Jeff Haden

AAA tenant Tenant with excellent credit who is considered unlikely to default on a lease. While a AAA tenant is unlikely to default on a lease, the fact they are rated as AAA is not a guarantee that prompt payments will be made.

Abandonment Voluntarily surrendering property that is either owned or leased without naming a successor as owner or tenant. An abandoned property tends to revert to the party holding a prior interest, such as a lender. Abandonment does not remove any obligations the person surrendering the property may have had, unless the entity owed those obligations agrees to waive those obligations. In simple terms, abandonment means, "I'm leaving, and I give up any rights to the property or its value...but I may still be liable for debts owed."

Abatement Abatement refers to a reduction of some kind. For instance, if the rent is decreased, that reduction constitutes an abatement. Abatement is also sometimes referred to as free rent or early occupancy.

Able A person who is financially capable of completing a real estate transaction; this does not imply the party is willing or ready to do so.

Abnormal sale A sale that does not represent a market transaction. If, for example, a house sells for $100,000 on a street where similar houses sell for $200,000, then the first home would be considered an abnormal sale. An appraiser may choose to disregard abnormal sales when selecting similar properties to compare values.

Above building standard Finishes or specialized designs that have been upgraded to accommodate a tenant's requirements.

Absentee owner An owner who does not reside in or personally manage a property. He may engage a property manager to oversee his rental properties.

Absorption rate The speed and amount of time at which rentable space, in square feet, is filled, or an estimate of the rate at which homes for sale will be purchased. For example, if a particular geographic area has 2,000 homes for sale and 200 are purchased each month, the area has an absorption rate of 10 percent (2,000 divided by 200.)

Abstract of judgment Document used to put bring about a judgment lien.

Abstract of title A summary of the history of a title to a particular parcel of real estate. It consists of a summary of the original grant and all subsequent conveyances and encumbrances affecting the property, and a certification by the abstractor that the history is complete and accurate.

Abstract update Adding copies of all relevant, new documents to an existing abstract of title to make the abstract of title current; frequently an abstract update is considered adequate for a property sale that occurs soon after a previous sale.

Abut To meet, join, or border. An abutment is the line where separate properties meet. A property can also abut a road, an easement, or other physical landmarks.

Accelerated Cost Recovery System (ACRS) A calculation for taxes to provide more depreciation for the first few years of ownership. Based on legislation from the Economic Recovery Tax Act, it sets forth requirements for how quickly property can be depreciated. For example, apartments can be depreciated over 27.5 years, and commercial property over 30 years.

Accelerated depreciation A method of depreciation where the value of a property depreciates faster in the first few years after purchasing it in order to increase the tax benefits of property ownership in those years.

Acceleration clause A clause in a contract that gives the lender the right to demand immediate payment of the balance of the loan if, for example, the borrower defaults on the loan. Other provisions could also trigger acceleration, depending on the terms of the original contract. For example, a loan agreement could contain an acceleration clause requiring immediate and full payment of the entire loan balance if a payment is more than 60 days overdue.

Acceptance Agreeing to accept an offer. If one party offers to buy a property at a specific price and under specific terms, and the owner agrees to those terms, then his or her acceptance means the sales contract is complete.

Accessibility The ease and convenience of entering a property by tenants, owners, customers, or any other users. Typically refers to foot traffic or automobile traffic, but could also refer to airplane traffic in subdivisions with accompanying landing strips for owners. A lack of accessibility typically results in a lower property value.

Accession Acquiring title to additions or improvements to real property as a result of the annexation of fixtures or the accretion of alluvial deposits along the banks of streams.

Accessory building A building that is used for another purpose besides the principal building on a lot. For example, a garage or outbuilding can be an accessory building. Typically does not refer to a separate building used for commercial purposes.

Accommodation party A person or persons who have signed an agreement without receiving value for that agreement. A loan cosigner, for example, is an accommodation party since the cosigner receives no value for having agreed to sign as a party on the loan.

Accord and satisfaction The settlement of an obligation. An accord is an agreement made by a creditor to accept something different from — or less than — what was originally promised. Once the creditor accepts an accord, the obligation of the debtor is removed. Typically an accord and satisfaction occurs when the two parties are in dispute.

Account payable The amount owed to a creditor by a debtor. Cash transactions do not result in accounts payable; any transaction where terms are offered do result in accounts payable. For example, a 30-day loan creates an account payable for the person who took out the loan.

Account receivable The amount a creditor is owed by a debtor. If a lender makes a 30-day loan to a creditor, the amount of the loan is considered an account receivable.

Accredited Management Organization (AMO) A designation given to management organizations that meet the standards set by the Institute of Real Estate Management.

Accredited Resident Manager (ARM) A designation given to management organizations that meet the standards set by the Institute of Real Estate Management. Given to qualified firms who specialize in managing residential properties.

Accretion The increase or addition of land by the deposit of sand or soil washed up naturally from a river, lake, or sea. This added land becomes the property of the landowner.

Accrual method An accounting method that requires income or expenses to be entered when the income is earned or the payment is payable. For example, if a property owner purchases a three-year insurance policy, under the accrual method, only the first year's insurance expense is shown as a journal entry, even if the property owner pays the entire balance in full.

Accrued depreciation The amount of depreciation expense that has been claimed to the present. Also referred to as accumulated depreciation.

Accrued items — Passive: On a closing statement, items of expense that are incurred but not yet payable, such as interest on a mortgage loan or taxes on real property. **Active:** Expenses prepaid within the current business year which must be imputed to the new business year. A rent prepayment entitles the company to use its rented facilities during the new business year.

Acknowledgment A formal declaration made before a duly authorized officer, usually a notary public, by a person who has signed a document. Documents requiring acknowledgement must be witnessed by an authorized officer like a notary public to become legal and enforceable.

Acquisition appraisal An appraisal to determine market value for a property acquired for public use by a government agency, usually through condemnation or negotiation. The purpose of an acquisition appraisal is to determine the amount the property owner will be compensated.

Acquisition cost The purchase price, including all fees, that will be necessary to obtain a property. The acquisition cost is the total cost to the buyer of the property.

Acre The standard of measurement for property. An acre is calculated in square feet or square yards. One acre equals 4,840 square yards, or 43,560 square feet.

Acreage zoning Zoning requirements that require large building lots in an effort to reduce residential or commercial density. Acreage zoning is sometimes called large-lot zoning or "snob zoning".

Act of God An act of nature beyond human control, including floods, hurricanes, lightning, and earthquakes. A contract can include an Act of God provision that relieves both parties of obligation where a natural disaster has destroyed or damaged the property.

Actual age The actual age of a property is its chronological age. Effective age refers to the state of the property. For example, a property with an actual age of 10 years may have an effective age of 20 years if upkeep and maintenance have not been performed.

Actual cash value Insurance term for the monetary value of an improvement. Actual cash value is determined by subtracting wear and tear from replacement cost.

Actual damages (and special damages) Damages that are a direct result of a wrong, recognizable by a court of law. If a doorway to a property is destroyed, actual damages are confined to the cost of repairing or replacing the doorway; special damages could be the loss of income or business due to the lack of a suitable entry to the property.

Actual eviction The process that results in the tenant's being physically removed from the leased premises.

Actual notice Express information or fact; that which is known; direct knowledge.

Ad valorem A Latin phrase which translated means "according to value." Ad valorem refers to a tax that is imposed on a property's value, typically based on the local government's evaluation of the property.

ADC loan A loan that covers the Acquisition, Development, and Construction of a development project. Its purpose is to allow the developer to purchase the land, put in streets and utility services, and construct buildings or houses.

Addendum An addition or update for an existing contract between parties. An addendum allows a revision to a contract without creating an entirely new contract. An addendum is only enforceable if both parties agree and sign.

Addition Construction that increases a building's size or significantly adds to it. Finishing previously unfinished space is not considered an addition, but is instead considered an improvement.

Additional principal payment Additional money paid to the lender, apart from the scheduled loan payments, to pay more of the principal balance, shortening the length of the loan.

Add-on interest Interest added to the principal of a loan regardless of repayment of principal. The borrower pays interest on the full principal balance for the entire loan period, not on the declining balance, even though the principal balance is reduced each month as payments are made. Add-on interest is sometimes referred to as "block interest."

Adjudication A court decision.

Adjunction The process of annexing one parcel of land to a larger parcel.

Adjustable Rate Mortgage (ARM) A home loan with an interest rate that is adjusted periodically to reflect changes in a specific financial resource; typically those changes are based on changes in mortgage loan interest rates, but changes can also be tied to government indexes or financial market indexes. Unlike a fixed-rate loan, the borrower's interest rate (and monthly payments) can change periodically based on the terms of the loan.

Adjusted Funds From Operations (AFFO) The rate of REIT performance or ability to pay dividends which is used by many analysts who have concerns about the quality of earnings as measured by Funds From Operations (FFO).

Adjustment date The date at which the interest rate is adjusted for an Adjustable Rate Mortgage (ARM).

Adjustment period The amount of time between adjustments for the interest rate in an Adjustable Rate Mortgage.

Advance fee A fee paid before services are rendered. For example, a real estate broker may require an advance fee to cover advertising expenses associated with marketing the property.

Advances Payments the servicer makes when the borrower fails to send a payment. For example, a second mortgagee may advance delinquent first mortgage payments to prevent a foreclosure of the secured property.

Adverse financial change condition Provisions in a loan agreement allowing the lender to cancel the agreement if the borrower suffers a major financial setback such as the loss of a job.

Adverse possession The actual, open, notorious, hostile, and continuous possession of another's land under a claim of title. Possession for a statutory period may be a means of acquiring title. Permission from the owner given in a lease would not constitute adverse possession because the possession is not hostile. For example, a person can gain title to land by living on the land for 20 years if the legal owner is unknown.

Adviser A broker or investment banker who represents an owner in a transaction and is paid a retainer and/or a performance fee once a financing or sales transaction has closed.

Aesthetic value Value of a property based on its appearance; for example, a lakefront property with a view of the lake may result in a higher sales price than comparable properties which do not afford the same view.

Affidavit of title A written statement, made under oath by a seller or grantor of real property and acknowledged by a notary public, in which the grantor (1) identifies himself or herself and indicates marital status, (2) certifies that since the examination of the title, on the date of the contracts no defects have occurred in the title, and (3) certifies that he or she is in possession of the property (if applicable).

Affirmation A declaration as to the truth of a statement. An affirmation is used in place of an oath; for example, when a person objects to swearing an oath for religious or personal reasons.

Affordability index A measurement of housing affordability compiled by the National Association of Realtors. The intent of the affordability index is to measure the ability of area residents to buy homes in that area.

Affordable housing A term frequently used to describe public and private efforts to help low-income individuals purchase homes. Typical programs include below-market interest rates, easier credit terms, or minimal down payments.

Age-life depreciation A technique for estimating all forms of depreciation sustained by an asset. The effective age of the property is divided by the economic life of the property. For example, if the roof of an income is effectively 5 years old, and it used a total economic life of 25 years, it is 20 percent (25 divided by 5) depreciated based on an age-life depreciation calculation.

Agency The relationship between a principal and an agent wherein the agent is authorized to represent the principal in certain transactions.

Agency closing A type of closing in which a lender uses a title company or other firm as an agent to complete a loan transaction.

Agency disclosure A requirement in most states that agents who act for both buyers or sellers must disclose who they are working for in the transaction. For example, a real estate agent working for the seller must provide an agency disclosure agreement notifying potential buyers that she is working on behalf of the sellers and not the buyer.

Agent One who acts or has the power to act for another. A fiduciary relationship is created under the law of agency when a property owner, as the principal, executes a listing agreement or management contract authorizing a licensed real estate broker to be his or her agent.

Aggrieved Suffering a loss or injury due to the infringement or denial of rights. Can also refer to an injured party who has lost personal or property rights.

Agreement of sale A legal document the buyer and seller must approve and sign that details the price and terms in the transaction.

Agricultural lien A loan advanced to a farmer to secure money or supplies for raising a crop. The lien attaches only to the crop, not to the land on which the crop is raised.

Air rights The right to control, use, or occupy the space above a specific property. Air rights can be sold, leased, or donated to another party. Air rights are not unlimited; while low-flying aircraft can be considered to be trespassing, aircraft flying at higher altitudes are not.

Alienation The act of transferring property to another. Alienation may be voluntary, such as by gift or sale, or involuntary, as through eminent domain or adverse possession.

Alienation clause The clause in a mortgage or deed of trust that states that the balance of the secured debt becomes immediately due and payable at the lender's option if the property is sold by the borrower. In effect this clause prevents the borrower from assigning the debt without the lender's approval.

Allodial system A legal system that gives full property ownership rights to individuals. The property rights system in the United States is based on the allodial system.

All-risks policy A property insurance policy that covers all hazards or perils except those specifically excluded in writing. In other words, if a hazard is not listed that hazard is covered by the policy.

Alluvion Soil deposited by accretion. Alluvion is typically considered to be the property of the property owner.

Alternative mortgage A home loan that does not match the standard terms of a fixed-rate mortgage. Examples of alternative mortgages are adjustable rate mortgages, rollover loans, graduated payment mortgages, and shared appreciation mortgages.

Alternative or specialty investments Types of property that are not considered to be conventional real estate investments, such as self-storage facilities, mobile homes, timber, agriculture, or parking lots.

Amenities Benefits derived from property ownership that are non-monetary. For example, a home in a prestigious neighborhood has an enhanced amenity of ownership. Amenities can also be features that increase a property's desirability, like custom fixtures or professional-grade appliances.

American Institute of Real Estate Appraisers Professional organization that promotes professional and ethical behavior among those in the real estate appraisal industry.

American Land Title Association (ALTA) policy A title insurance policy that protects the interest in a collateral property of a mortgage lender who originates a new real estate loan. ALTA promotes uniformity and quality in title abstract and title insurance policies.

American standard A standard used for the measurement of office space that can be occupied by the tenant for furnishings and employees.

Americans with Disabilities Act Addresses rights of individuals with disabilities in employment and public accommodations. Designed to eliminate discrimination against individuals with disabilities by requiring equal access to jobs, public accommodations, government services, public transportation, and telecommunications. Includes the design of buildings intended to serve the public.

Amortization The usual process of paying a loan's interest and principal via scheduled monthly payments. Simply put, amortization is the gradual paying off of a debt by making periodic installment payments.

Amortization schedule A chart or table which shows the percentage of each payment that will be applied toward principal and interest over the life of the mortgage and how the loan balance decreases until it reaches zero.

Amortization tables The mathematical tables that are used to calculate what a borrower's monthly payment will be. An amortization schedule shows the payment, interest and principal breakdown, and unpaid loan balance for each period of the life of a loan.

Amortization term The number of months it will take to amortize (pay off) the loan.

Amortized loan A loan in which the principal as well as the interest is payable in monthly or other periodic installments over the term of the loan. An interest-only loan, where payments are only applied to accrued interest, is not an amortized loan.

Anchor tenant The business or individual who is serving as the primary draw to a commercial property. For example, a large department store located at the end of a shopping center may be considered the anchor tenant of the center.

Annexation The process whereby a city expands its boundaries to include a specific geographic area. Most states require a public vote be held within the city and the area to be annexed in order to determine public approval. Annexation can also refer to the process where personal property becomes attached to real property.

Annual debt service The required annual principal and interest payments for a loan. If a loan requires principal payments of $300 and interest payments of $50 per month, then the annual debt service of the loan is $4,200 ($350 times 12.)

Annual mortgagor statement A yearly statement to borrowers detailing the remaining principal balance and amounts paid throughout the year for taxes and interest. Used by mortgagees for tax purposes and to determine loan status.

Annual Percentage Rate (APR) The effective rate of interest for a loan per year; this disclosure is required by the Truth in Lending Law. The annual percentage rate is generally higher than the advertised interest rate.

Annuity Regular payments of a fixed sum.

Anticipation The appraisal principle that holds that value can increase or decrease based on the expectation of some future benefit or detriment produced by the property. An appraiser can determine that the value of property today is the present value of the sum of anticipated future benefits. If an income property is determined to be likely to be worthless at a specific time in the future, its present value may be adjusted to reflect that anticipated future value.

Antitrust laws Laws designed to preserve the free enterprise of the open marketplace by making illegal certain private conspiracies and combinations formed to minimize competition. Most violations of antitrust laws in the real estate business involve either price-fixing (brokers conspiring to set fixed compensation rates) or allocation of customers or markets (brokers agreeing to limit their areas of trade or dealing to certain areas or properties).

Apartment building A dwelling unit within a multi-family structure, usually provided as rental housing. Apartment buildings are usually multi-family dwellings with individual living units but a common entranceway or hallway.

Application The form a borrower must complete to apply for services like a mortgage loan or to rent a dwelling; often includes information like income, savings, assets, debts, and references.

Application fee A fee some lenders charge that may include fees for items such as property appraisal or a credit report (unless those fees are included elsewhere).

Appointments Furnishings, fixtures, or equipment found in a home or other building. The items can increase or decrease the usability and/or value of the property.

Apportionment Prorating property expenses, like taxes and insurance, between the buyer and the seller of a property. Typically used to divide yearly costs between the two parties. For example, if a property is purchased on July 1, the seller may pay 50 percent of the tax liability for that year, and the buyer will be responsible for the other 50 percent.

Appraisal The estimate of the value of a property on a particular date given by a professional appraiser, usually presented in a written document.

Appraisal fee The fee charged by a professional appraiser for estimating the market value of a property.

Appraisal report The written report presented by an appraiser regarding the value of a property; should include a description and summary of the method(s) used to calculate the value of the property.

Appraised value The dollar amount a professional appraiser assigns to the value of a property in an appraisal report.

Appraiser A certified individual who is qualified by education, training, and experience to estimate the value of real and personal property.

Appreciation An increase in the value of a home or property. Appreciation can be due to inflation, physical additions or changes, changes to market values, and other causes.

Appropriation To set aside land for public use. For example, a developer of a new subdivision may be required to apportion land for a new school to gain approval to begin the project.

Appurtenance A right, privilege, or improvement belonging to and passing with the land. An appurtenance is something outside the property itself but is considered a part of the property that adds to its greater enjoyment, like the right to cross another party's land. (Easements and rights-of-way are considered to be appurtenances.)

Appurtenant easement An easement that is annexed to the ownership of one parcel and allows the owner the use of the neighbor's land.

Arbitrage The act of buying securities in one market and selling them immediately in another market to profit from the difference in price.

Arbitration Settling disputes through a neutral third party. Arbitration is typically an alternative to filing suit in a court of law. Many real estate sales contracts contain a provision requiring both parties to submit their disputes to arbitration, as a result, both parties have waived their right to filing suit in a public court.

Architecture The manner in which a building is constructed, including the floor plan, style, appearance, materials used, and building technologies used.

Area A two-dimensional space. Can refer to a floor area or the area of a lot. For example, a room that measures ten feet by ten feet has an area of 100 square feet (10 times 10 = 100.)

ARM index A number that is publicly published and used as the basis for interest rate adjustments on an ARM.

Arm's length transaction A transaction among parties where each party acts in his or her own best interests. For example, typically a transaction between a husband and a wife would not be considered arm's length.

Arrears At the end of a term. For example, interest on a mortgage loan is usually paid in arrears, meaning at the end of a month or other period. Arrears is also sometimes used to signify a default or late payment. If a homeowner has not made mortgage payments for two months, his mortgage can be considered to be in arrears.

Artesian well A shaft that reaches water that rises because of natural underground pressure.

"As is" condition A phrase in a purchase or lease contract in which the buyer accepts the existing condition of the premises as well as the presence of any physical defects. "As is" sales provide no guarantees to the buyer. If a property owner sells a home "as is," the buyer cannot demand repairs to non-working appliances, for example.

Asbestos A mineral once used in insulation and other materials that can cause respiratory diseases.

Asbestos Containing Materials (ACM) Products or materials made with asbestos. Use of ACMs has been prohibited since the early 1980s, but some older dwellings still may contain ACMs.

As-built drawings Architectural drawings showing the precise method of construction and the location of equipment and utilities. As-built drawings reflect any changes to the original plans.

Asking price The list price an owner would like to receive. The asking price is not necessarily the owner's bottom-line price. Asking price can also be described as "advertised price".

Assemblage Combining two or more adjoining lots into one larger tract to increase the total value.

Assessed value The value placed on a home, determined by a tax assessor to calculate a tax base.

Assessment The estimated value of a piece of real estate or a special levy placed in addition to taxes.

Assessment rolls The public record of the assessed value of a property in a jurisdiction. The assessment roll of a town shows the total assessed value (with an individual breakdown of values) of all the properties within the town.

Assessor A public officer who estimates the value of a property for the purpose of taxation.

Asset A property or item of value.

Asset Depreciation Range system (ADR) Internal Revenue Service regulations defining the standards for determining the period of time over which an asset can be depreciated. The ADR gives taxpayers a choice of depreciating the property over a shorter or longer life than the standard guideline period.

Asset management The various tasks and areas involved in managing real estate assets from the time of initial investment until the time it is sold.

Asset management fee A fee charged to investors based on the amount of money they have invested in real estate assets for the particular fund or account. Asset management fees are usually calculated on a percentage basis.

Assets under management The amount of the current market value of real estate assets which a manager is responsible for managing and investing.

Assignee The individual or business to whom the lease, mortgage, or other contract has been re-assigned.

Assignment The transfer of rights and responsibilities from one party to another. The original party remains liable for debt should the second party default, however. A lease is an example of an assignment, since it gives another individual the right to use the leased space. While the tenant may pay rent, the owner is still responsible for making any loan payments.

Assignment of lease Transfer of rights to use a leased property from one leasing party to another. For example, a college student who does not need an apartment during the summer months may assign the lease to another party for that time period.

Assignment of rents A contract that assigns rents from the tenant of a property to the mortgage lender in case of a default. Some lenders require an assignment of rents.

Assignor The person who transfers the rights and interests of a property to another.

Associate broker A licensed broker whose license is held by another broker. An associate broker qualifies to be a real estate broker but still works for and is supervised by another broker. Associate brokers are sometimes called broker-associates, broker-salespersons, or affiliate brokers.

Association of unit owners Unit owners of a condominium who act as a group for administering the property. Condominium Owners' Associations are considered an association of unit owners.

Assumable mortgage A mortgage that is capable of being transferred to a different borrower.

Assumption The act of assuming the mortgage of a seller.

Assumption clause A contractual provision that enables the buyer to take responsibility for the mortgage loan from the seller.

Assumption fee A fee charged to the buyer assuming an existing loan for processing new documents and agreements.

Assumption of mortgage Acquiring title to property on which there is an existing mortgage and agreeing to be personally liable for the terms and conditions of the mortgage, including payments. Fees are typically set at the time of loan origination.

At risk rules Tax laws that limit the amount of tax losses an investor can claim. Losses on real estate investments are limited to the amount of money an investor stands to lose.

Attachment The act of taking a person's property into legal custody by writ or other judicial order to hold it available for application to that person's debt to a creditor. Attachment is the legal seizure of property to force payment of a debt; for example, a landlord may attach a tenant's personal property to force payment of back rent.

Attest To witness by observation and signature; a third party, who has witnessed the signing of a document by its principles, will attest to the signing.

Attic Accessible space between the ceiling of the top floor and the structure's roof. Inaccessible space is considered to be a structural cavity and not an attic.

Attorn To agree to recognize a new owner of a property and to pay rent to the new landlord.

Attorney-in-fact Person who is authorized to act for another person under a power of attorney. A son who has power of attorney to sell a father's property is considered to be the attorney-in-fact.

Attorney's opinion of title An abstract of title that an attorney has examined and has certified to be, in his or her opinion, an accurate statement of the facts concerning the property ownership. In short, the attorney has judged the title to a particular party to be good.

Attornment A tenant's formal agreement to be a tenant of a new landlord. For example, if a previous landlord defaults and the property is foreclosed upon, the new owner may ask all tenants to sign a letter of attornment indicating they recognize the new landlord.

Attractive nuisance An appealing but possibly hazardous or dangerous feature of a property that can lure trespassers who could then suffer harm. By law, the owner of an attractive nuisance must take special measures to avoid liability. For example, many localities require fencing over a specific height to protect swimming pools from trespassers.

Auction To sell land or personal property by inviting bidders. The property is sold to the highest bidder. Bids can either be written or verbal and public or private. Many states require that foreclosed properties be auctioned.

Auctioneer Person who conducts an auction; usually requires licensing, especially where real estate auctions are concerned.

Authorization to sell A listing contract giving an agent the right to find a buyer for a property. The agent is not permitted to enter into an agreement for sale; the agent is allowed to market the property for sale and is entitled to compensation for finding a buyer.

Automated underwriting Computer systems that permit lenders to expedite the loan approval process and reduce lending costs.

Automatic extension A clause in a listing agreement stating that the agreement will continue automatically for a specific period of time after its expiration date. In many states the use of this clause is discouraged or prohibited.

Average downtime The number of months anticipated between a lease's expiration and the beginning of a replacement lease under current market conditions. If a property is expected to take three months to lease after the previous tenant vacates, the average downtime is three months.

Average free rent The number of months the rent abatement concession is expected to be granted to a tenant as part of an incentive to lease under current market conditions. This figure can increase or decrease based on supply and demand and other economic factors.

Average occupancy The average rate of each of the previous 12 months that a property was occupied. A property occupied for 11 of the past 12 months is considered to have an average occupancy of 92 percent (11 divided by 12.)

Avulsion The sudden removal of land from one place to another. Can be caused by factors like massive erosion or when a river abruptly changes its course. Avulsion is the opposite of accretion.

Back end ratio The calculation lenders use to compare a borrower's gross monthly income to their total debt when determining loan approval. Takes into account existing long-term debt.

Back title letter A letter an attorney receives from a title insurance company before examining the title for insurance purposes.

Backfill Replacement of excavated dirt into a hole or against a structure.

Backup offer An offer to buy or lease real estate that becomes effective if a prior contract falls through. For example, a buyer may make a backup offer on a property already under contract to another party in the hopes that the other party will be unable to purchase the property.

Balance The amount remaining to be paid toward an obligation. For example, a homeowner who has paid down $25,000 of a $100,000 mortgage has a principal balance of $75,000. Balance also refers to the appraisal principle that states the greatest value in a property will occur when the type and size of the improvements are proportional to each other as well as the land.

Balance sheet A statement that lists an individual's assets, liabilities, and net worth.

Balloon loan A type of mortgage in which the monthly payments are not large enough to repay the loan by the end of the term, and the final payment is a large payment that covers the remainder of the obligation. A balloon loan may call for monthly payments of $1,000 per month for 5 years, with a final payment of $100,000.

Balloon payment A final payment of a mortgage loan that is considerably larger than the required periodic payments because the loan amount was not fully amortized.

Balloon risk The risk that a borrower may not be able to come up with the funds for the balloon payment at maturity.

Bankruptcy The financial inability to pay debts when they are due. The debtor seeks relief through court actions that may modify or erase his or her debts.

Bargain and sale deed A deed that carries with it no warranties against liens or other encumbrances but that does imply that the grantor has the right to convey title. The grantor may add warranties to the deed at his or her discretion. A bargain and sale deed is one in which the grantor of the deed implies to have an interest in the property but offers no warranties of clear title.

Base loan amount The amount which forms the basis for the loan payments.

Base principal balance The original loan amount once adjustments for subsequent fundings and principal payments have been made without including accrued interest or other unpaid debts.

Base rent An amount that is used as a minimum rent, providing for rent increases over the term of the lease agreement. The base rent is the initial rent, and depending on the lease provisions it may change over the term of the lease. In commercial properties, the base rent is the minimum due each month, with extra payments due based on, for example, a percentage of sales. A retail store may have a base rent of $500 per month, with an additional rent amount of 2 percent of gross sales.

Basis The financial interest that the Internal Revenue Service attributes to an owner of an investment property for the purpose of determining annual depreciation and gain or loss on the sale of the asset. If a property was acquired by purchase, the owner's basis is the cost of the property plus the value of any capital expenditures for improvements to the property, minus any depreciation allowable or actually taken. This new basis is called the adjusted basis.

Basis point A term for 1/100 of one percentage point. Typically used by the financial markets. For example, if interest rates decrease from 5.25 percent to 5.15 percent, the reduction is 10 basis points (5.25 minus 5.15).

Before and after method The practice of appraising a property before and after it has been taken through eminent domain. The appraiser calculates the property before the seizure, and then after, to take into account any increases or decreases in value due to the change in use. The before and after method typically results in a lower appraised value.

Before tax income An individual or company's income before taxes have been deducted.

Below grade Any structure or part of a structure that is below the surface of the ground that surrounds it.

Bench mark A permanently affixed mark that establishes exact elevation; surveyors use benchmarks to measure site elevations or as starting points for surveys.

Beneficiary A beneficiary is a person who receives or is entitled to receive the benefits resulting from certain acts. A beneficiary can be a person for whom a trust operates or in whose behalf the income from a trust estate is drawn. The term beneficiary also refers to a lender in a deed of trust loan transaction.

Benefits The enhancements gained from a public improvement of a property taken in an eminent domain proceeding. A benefit could be a new school, a new highway, or a new public project. Benefits typically are general, meaning they enhance all properties in the area.

Bequeath To specify by will the recipient of personal property; does not apply to real estate. (To devise is to specify the recipient of real estate.)

Beta The measurement of common stock price volatility for a company in comparison to the market.

Betterment An improvement to real estate. If a property owner constructs a building on a lot, the building is considered a betterment to the property.

Bid The price or range an investor is willing to spend on whole loans or securities.

Bilateral contract A contract where each party promises performance. For example, the sale of a home is a bilateral contract; the seller promises to convey the home, and the buyer promises to pay an agreed-upon price.

Bill of sale A written legal document that transfers the ownership of personal property to another party. A bill of sale does not convey title of real estate — it is only used for transferring ownership of personal property.

Binder An agreement that may accompany an earnest money deposit for the purchase of real property as evidence of the purchaser's good faith and intent to complete the transaction. A binder is not a contract; it signifies intent to join a contract.

Biweekly mortgage A mortgage repayment plan that requires payments every two weeks to help repay the loan over a shorter amount of time. The payments are exactly half of what a monthly payment would be, but at the end of the year the borrower will have made 26 payments, or the equivalent of 13 monthly payments, causing the loan to be paid off more quickly.

Blanket loan A mortgage covering more than one parcel of real estate, providing for each parcel's partial release from the mortgage lien upon repayment of a definite portion of the debt.

Blended rate An interest rate applied to a refinanced loan that is higher than the rate of the old loan but lower than the current rate offered on new loans. Blended rates are usually offered by lenders as incentives for borrowers to refinance existing low-interest rate loans instead of offering a purchaser the chance to assume the loan. For example, if current rates are 10 percent, and a buyer can assume a loan at 7 percent, the lender may offer 8 percent financing to entice the buyer to get new financing instead of assuming the old mortgage.

Blighted areas A section of a city or locality where a majority of the structures are dilapidated or in poor condition.

Blind pool A mixed fund that accepts capital from investors without specifying property assets. Investors contribute to the blind pool without knowing which properties will be purchased.

Blockbusting The illegal practice of inducing homeowners to sell their properties by making representations regarding the entry or prospective entry of persons of a particular race or national origin into the neighborhood.

Blue laws Laws restricting the transaction of business on Sundays and/or certain religious holidays.

Blueprint A detailed, working set of plans used as the guide for construction for a building or structure.

Board of directors Persons elected by stockholders to govern a corporation. In most states at least two persons are needed to constitute a board.

Board of Realtors® Group of real estate license holders who are members of the state and National Association of Realtors®.

Boiler plate Standard language found in contracts; usually refers to pre-printed, mass distribution documents. The phrase "boiler plate language" is used to imply "standard".

Bona fide In good faith, without fraud. A notarized contract is considered to be a bona fide contract, since a third-party has verified the identities of the signors.

Book value The value of a property based on its purchase amount, plus upgrades or other additions, with depreciation subtracted. Book value is typically used by corporations to show the value of properties they own.

Boot Money or property given to make up any difference in value or equity between two properties in an exchange.

Bottomland Low land near a river, lake, or stream which is often flooded. Also refers to land in a valley.

Boundary A property line; describes the outer edge of a property.

Branch office A secondary place of business apart from the principal or main office from which real estate business is conducted. A branch office usually must be run by a licensed real estate broker working on behalf of the broker.

Breach of contract Violation of any terms or conditions in a contract without legal excuse; for example, failure to make a payment when it is due is considered a breach of contract.

Break-even point The point at which a landlord's income from rent matches expenses and debt. If the total of rents and income equals the total of payments and expenses, the property is at the break-even point.

Bridge loan Mortgage financing between the end of one loan and the beginning of another loan, or a short-term loan for individuals or companies who are still seeking more permanent financing. Bridge loans are frequently used during a property's construction phase. A bridge loan is sometimes referred to as a gap loan or a swing loan.

Bring down search An extension of a title search to verify that no liens have been filed against the property between the time of the original title search and the recording of the deed or mortgage. In most states, the buyer typically pays the fee for a bring-down search.

British Thermal Unit (BTU) A unit of heat; one BTU is the energy required to raise the temperature of one pound of water by one degree Fahrenheit. The output of most heating systems is measured in BTUs.

Broker A person who serves as a go-between between a buyer and seller, typically for a commission.

Brokerage The business of being a broker; usually refers to the company or organization run by a broker.

Brownfield A site whose former use involved hazardous materials. Examples are shut down military bases, abandoned gas stations, or shut down manufacturing facilities.

Brownstone A three to five story row house with common walls for adjoining properties.

Budget mortgage A mortgage involving payments totaling more than interest and principal; typically includes additions for property taxes, insurance, or other fees that, if not paid, could result in foreclosure. A budget mortgage is commonly used in VA, FHA, and conventional residential mortgages. Additional funds are held by the lender in an escrow account until payment is required.

Buffer zone A strip of land, usually used as a park or designated for a similar use, separating land dedicated to one use from land dedicated to another use; for example, separating residential properties from commercial properties.

Build out Improvements to a property that have been made according to a tenant's specifications.

Build to suit A way of leasing property, usually for commercial purposes, in which the developer or landlord builds to a tenant's specifications. The landowner pays for the construction to the specifications of the tenant, and the tenant then leases the land and building from the landowner, who retains ownership. Build to suit is frequently used by tenants who wish to occupy a building of a certain type but do not wish to own the building.

Buildable acres The portion of land that can be built upon after allowances for roads, setbacks, anticipated open spaces, and unsuitable areas have been made.

Building code The laws set forth by the local government regarding end use of a given piece of property. These laws code may dictate the design, materials used, and/or types of improvements that will be allowed. New construction or improvements must meet building code; adherence to requirements is determined by building inspectors.

Building line Lines a specified distance from the sides of a lot that denote where a building cannot be placed. Building lines are often called setbacks, because a building must be "set back" a specified distance from the property line.

Building permit Written permission for the construction, alteration, or demolition of an improvement; shows compliance with building codes and zoning ordinances.

Building restrictions Provisions and specifications in building codes that affect the placement, size, and appearance of a building. Building restrictions include building lines, the allowable height of a structure, and other provisions.

Building standards Specific elements of construction an owner or developer chooses to use throughout a building. Building standards offered to a tenant of a leased office; for example, might include the types of doors, ceilings, light fixtures, carpet, and other features.

Bulk sale The sale of a group or collection of real estate assets, usually different properties in different locations. A bulk sale requires the buyer to accept all properties.

Bullet loan A loan with a 5- to 10-year term and no amortization (no monthly payments). At the end of the term the full amount of principal and accumulated interest is due.

Bundle of legal rights The concept of land ownership that includes ownership of all legal rights to the land; for example, possession, control within the law, and enjoyment.

Bureau of Land Management The agency of the United States government that oversees the management of the majority of the land owned by the government, specifically national parks and undeveloped land.

Bureau rate A standard rate for hazard insurance, and for title insurance in some states, established by a rating bureau for all companies writing policies in that particular area.

Business day A standard day for conducting business; excludes weekends and holidays.

Business interruption insurance Insurance that covers financial damages that occur as a result of repairs needed to a building due to a fire or other insured hazard. Many retail stores carry business interruption insurance, as do large apartment complexes.

Buy back agreement A provision in a contract where the seller agrees to repurchase the property at a stated price if a specified event occurs. For example, a builder could be required to buy back a retail property at a specific price if certain sales thresholds are not met.

Buydown A financing technique used to reduce the monthly payments for the first few years of a loan. Funds in the form of discount points are given to the lender by the builder or seller to buy down or lower the effective interest rate paid by the buyer, thus reducing the monthly payments for a set time.

Buydown mortgage A type of home loan in which the lender receives a higher payment in order to convince them to reduce the interest rate during the initial years of the mortgage.

Buyer's agent A residential real estate salesperson who represents the prospective purchaser in a transaction. The buyer's agent owes the buyer/principal the common-law or statutory agency duties. Similar to a buyer's broker.

Buyer's broker A residential real estate broker who represents prospective buyers exclusively. As the buyer's agent, the broker owes the buyer/principal the common-law or statutory agency duties. Similar to a buyer's agent.

Buyers' market A condition where buyers have a wide choice of properties and may negotiate lower prices. Buyer's markets occur when there are more houses for sale than there are buyers. Buyers' markets can be caused by factors like overbuilding, an economic downturn, or a decrease in the local population.

Buyer's remorse The nervousness some first-time homebuyers may feel after signing a sales contract or closing on the purchase of a house.

Cadastral map A legal map for recording ownership of property. The map describes both the boundaries and the ownership of properties.

Call provision A clause in the loan agreement that allows a lender to demand repayment of the entire principal balance at any time if loan provisions are not met; for example, a lender can exercise the call provision if the buyer is more than sixty days late on payments.

Cancellation clause A contract provision that allows the termination of obligation if certain conditions or events occur. For example, a cancellation clause in a lease can allow the landlord to break the lease if he or she sells the property.

Cap A limit on how much the monthly payment or interest rate is allowed to increase in an adjustable rate mortgage. Designed to protect the borrower from large increases in the interest rate which would naturally result in large increases to the monthly payment amount.

Capacity of parties A valid contract requires that all parties be legally able to enter into the agreement. Capacity of parties is one of the requirements for a valid and binding contract.

Minors, the mentally insane, and persons who are under the influence are not considered to be of legal capacity to enter into a contract.

Capital Money used to purchase long-term assets. In real estate terms, capital is cash — or the ability to turn an asset into cash. A person who does not have sufficient capital does not have enough cash (or liquid assets that can be turned into cash).

Capital appreciation An increase in the value of a property after it has been adjusted for capital improvements and partial sales. Capital appreciation refers to the value of a property; a capital gain is realized when the property is actually sold.

Capital assets Assets that the Internal Revenue Service defines as such; includes properties or equipment. An income property is considered a capital asset.

Capital expenditures The purchase of long-term assets, or the expansion of existing ones which prolongs the life or efficiency of those assets.

Capital gain The amount of excess when the net proceeds from the sale of an asset are higher than its book value. If a buyer purchases a property for $200,000 and sells it after three years for $300,000 he or she has experienced a capital gain of $100,000.

Capital improvements Expenses that prolong the life of a property or add improvements to it. Buying a lawn mower is not considered a capital improvement, but constructing a building on a lot is a capital improvement.

Capital loss Loss from the sale of a capital asset. If the sale price is less than the purchase price plus other capital expenses, the owner has suffered a capital loss.

Capital markets Public and private markets where individuals or businesses can raise or borrow capital.

Capitalization A mathematical process for estimating the value of a property using a proper rate of return on the investment and the annual net operating income expected to be produced by the property. The formula is value equals annual income divided by capitalization rate.

Capitalization rate The percentage of return determined from the net income of a property and its underlying value. A property valued at $100,000 with a net operating income of $10,000 has a capitalization rate of 10 percent.

Carryback financing A type of funding in which a seller agrees to hold back a note for a specified portion of the sales price. For example, a buyer with no down payment funds available may arrange for 80 percent financing from a primary lender, with the seller offering to loan him the other 20 percent as carryback financing. The carryback financing in this case is the junior or secondary lien.

Carrying charges Costs incurred to the landlord when initially leasing out a property and then during the periods of vacancy.

Cash equivalent The conversion of the price of a property that sold with favorable or unfavorable financing into the price the property would have sold for if the seller accepted all cash. If the financing is unfavorable for the seller, then the sale price he received is reduced; if the financing is favorable for the seller, then the sale price is adjusted upwards.

Cash flow The net income from an investment determined by deducting all operating and fixed expenses from the gross income. If expenses exceed income a negative cash flow results.

Cash method An accounting method based on cash receipts and cash expenditures. For accounting purposes, income and expenses are booked when monies are received and spent, not when they are due.

Cash on cash yield The percentage of a property's net cash flow and the average amount of invested capital during the specified operating year.

Cash out To completely liquidate an asset. Also refers to a mortgage refinance where a borrower takes cash out of the equity of the property. For example, a borrower owing $100,000 on a property valued at $200,000 who takes a new mortgage of $150,000 has taken $50,000 cash out of the property.

Cash rent In an agricultural lease, the amount of money given as rent to the landowner at the beginning of the lease, as opposed to sharecropping.

Cashier's check A check the bank draws on its own resources instead of a depositor's account. A cashier's check is preferred (and frequently required) in real estate transactions, because the bank guarantees payment.

Cash-out refinance The act of refinancing a mortgage for an amount that is higher than the original amount for the purpose of using the remaining cash for personal use.

Caveat emptor A Latin phrase meaning "Let the buyer beware." The buyer is responsible for inspecting the property or item and is assumed to be buying at his or her own risk.

Cease and desist order An order by a court or agency prohibiting a person or business from continuing an activity. Used in real estate to prevent antitrust behavior among firms, or to put a stop to illegal discrimination.

Central business district The downtown section of a city, generally consisting of retail, office, hotel, entertainment, and high density housing.

Certificate of completion A document issued by an architect or engineer stating that a property meets all specifications listed on the original plans and blueprints. Many construction contracts specify that final payment must be made when a certificate of completion has been signed.

Certificate of Deposit Index (CODI) A rate based on the interest rate of six-month CDs; often used as the index to determine interest rates for ARMs.

Certificate of Eligibility (COE) A document issued by the Veterans Administration (VA) to verify the eligibility of a veteran for a VA loan.

Certificate of insurance A document issued by an insurance company to verify coverage. Most lending institutions require a certificate of insurance proving the borrower is carrying adequate insurance to cover the subject property.

Certificate of Occupancy (CO) A written document issued by a local government or building agency that states that a home or building is habitable after meeting all building codes. Indicates the building is in compliance with health and building requirements.

Certificate of Reasonable Value (CRV) An appraisal presented by the Veterans Administration (VA) that shows the current market value of a property.

Certificate of sale The document generally given to the purchaser at a tax foreclosure sale. A certificate of sale does not convey title; normally it is an instrument certifying that the holder received title to the property after the redemption period passed and that the holder paid the property taxes for that interim period.

Certificate of title A statement of opinion on the status of the title to a parcel of real property based on an examination of specified public records; typically given by an attorney after a title search.

Certificate of Veteran Status A document veterans or reservists receive if they have served 90 days of continuous active duty (including training time).

Certified check A check the bank draws on a customer's account on which the bank has noted its certification. A cashier's check is preferred (and frequently required) in real estate transactions, because the bank guarantees payment.

Certified general appraiser A person qualified to appraise any property. Requires at least 3,000 hours of general appraisal experience, plus a 4-year college degree or 30 semester hours of specified college work, 300 hours of education, and passing a state examination.

Certified Property Manager A professional designation given by to real estate managers by the Institute of Real Estate Management.

Chain of title The history of conveyances, from some accepted starting point, whereby the present holder of real property derives title. The chain of title is used to prepare an attorney's opinion of title as to whether the owner has a marketable or insurable interest in the property (in other words, a clear title.)

Change order Instructions to revise construction plans after plans have been completed and construction is under way. Change orders almost always result in increased cost.

Chattel Personal property. Chattel is anything owned and tangible other than real estate. Furniture, cars, jewelry, and clothing are all examples of chattel.

Chattel mortgage A pledge of personal property as security for a debt. A person who borrows money using jewelry as a security has entered into a chattel mortgage.

Circulation factor The interior space of a structure that is required for internal office circulation and is not included in the net square footage.

Civil Rights Act of 1866 An act that prohibits racial discrimination in the sale and rental of housing.

Class "A" A rating usually assigned to properties that will generate the maximum rent per square foot, due to superior quality and/or location.

Class "B" A rating usually assigned to a property that most potential tenants would find desirable but lacks certain attributes that would result in maximum rents per square foot.

Class "C" A rating usually assigned to a property that is physically acceptable but offers few amenities; as a result the rent per square foot will be low.

Clear span Term used to describe an open area with no obstructions. For example, a warehouse with a 20-foot ceiling can store more items than a warehouse with a 10-foot ceiling.

Clear span facility A type of building, usually a warehouse or parking garage, consisting of vertical columns on the outer edges of the structure and clear spaces between the columns.

Clear title A property title that is free of liens, defects, or other legal encumbrances.

Clearance letter A letter from a licensed termite inspector showing the results of a termite inspection. Many loans, including FHA and VA loans, require a clearance letter before approving a mortgage.

Closed end mortgage A mortgage loan whose principal amount cannot be increased during the payout period. Most first mortgages provide the full balance at loan origination; no additional funds will be disbursed.

Closing The final act of procuring a loan and title in which documents are signed between the buyer and seller and/ or their respective representation, and all money and consideration changes hands.

Closing costs Expenses related to the sale of real estate including the loan, title, and appraisal fees; does not include the price of the property itself.

Closing statement Detailed cash accounting of a real estate transaction showing all cash received, all charges and credits made, and all cash paid out as a result of the transaction.

Cloud on title Refers to any document, claim, unreleased lien, or encumbrance that may impair the title to real property or make the title doubtful. A cloud on title is usually revealed by a title search and removed by either a quitclaim deed or suit to quiet title; in some instance, however, the clouds cannot be removed quickly.

Cluster housing A subdivision technique where dwellings are grouped close together with a common area left for recreation. In effect residents have extremely small yards but can enjoy the large common spaces.

Clustering Grouping home sites within a subdivision on smaller lots than normal, with the remaining land used as common areas.

Co-borrower Another individual who is jointly responsible for the loan and is on the title to the property. A co-signer typically is not on the title to the property.

Code of ethics A written system of standards for ethical conduct. For example, all Realtors® are required to follow a code of ethics that defines professional behavior.

Codicil A supplement or an addition to a will, executed with the same formalities as a will that normally does not revoke the entire will.

Coinsurance clause A clause in insurance policies covering real property that requires the policyholder to maintain fire insurance coverage generally equal to at least 80 percent of the property's actual replacement cost.

Co-investment The condition that occurs when two or more pension funds or groups of funds are sharing ownership of a real estate investment.

Co-investment program A separate account for an insurance company or investment partnership in which two or more pension funds may co-invest their capital in an individual property or a portfolio of properties.

Collateral The property for which a borrower has obtained a loan, thereby assuming the risk of losing the property if the loan is not repaid according to the terms of the loan agreement.

Collateralized Mortgage Obligation (CMO) Debt that is fully based on a pool of mortgages. A CMO is a security that is backed by a pool of mortgage loans.

Collection The effort on the part of a lender, due to a borrower's defaulting on a loan, which involves mailing and recording certain documents in the event that the foreclosure procedure must be implemented.

Color of title A title which appears to be a good title, but is not. For example, a seller could give a buyer title to a property that he does not own; the buyer would take possession under a color of title — in other words, the buyer thinks and acts as if he has clear title, but in actuality he does not.

Commercial acre The portion of commercial land that can be built upon after allowances for roads, setbacks, anticipated open spaces, and unsuitable areas have been made.

Commercial leasehold insurance Insurance to cover the payment of rent in the event the insured tenant cannot pay. Some commercial lenders require commercial leasehold insurance in shopping centers.

Commercial mortgage A loan used to purchase a piece of commercial property or building.

Commercial mortgage broker A broker specialized in commercial mortgage applications.

Commercial mortgage lender A lender specialized in funding commercial mortgage loans.

Commercial Mortgage-Backed Securities (CMBS) A type of security that is backed by loans on commercial real estate.

Commercial property Property designed for use by retail, wholesale, office, hotel, or other service businesses. Commercial properties are typically not long-term residential structures.

Commingled fund A pooled fund that enables qualified employee benefit plans to mix their capital to achieve professional management, greater diversification, or investment positions in larger properties.

Commingling The illegal act by a real estate broker or agent where the agent places client or customer funds into an account with his or her own funds. By law, brokers are required to maintain a separate trust or escrow account for other parties' funds held temporarily by the broker. For example, earnest money provided with an offer must be deposited in a separate account.

Commission Payment to a broker for services rendered, such as in the sale or purchase of real property; usually a percentage of the selling price of the property.

Commitment The agreement of a lender to make a loan with given terms for a specific period.

Commitment fee The fee a lender charges for the guarantee of specified loan terms, to be honored at some point in the future. The commitment fee is required to lock in specific terms on a loan at the time of application.

Common area assessments Sometimes called Homeowners' Association Fees. Charges paid to the Homeowners' Association by the individual unit owners, in a condominium or Planned Unit Development (PUD), that are usually used to maintain the property and common areas.

Common Area Maintenance (CAM) Charges (over and above rent) to tenants for expenses to maintain hallways, restrooms, parking lots, playgrounds, and other common areas.

Common areas The portions of a building, land, and amenities, owned or managed by a planned unit development (PUD) or condominium's homeowners' association, that are used by all of the unit owners who share in the common expense of operation and maintenance.

Common elements Parts of a property that are necessary or convenient to the existence, maintenance, and safety of a condominium or are normally in common use by all of the condominium residents. Each condominium owner has an undivided ownership interest in the common elements.

Common law The body of law based on custom, usage, and court decisions. Common law prevails unless superseded by other law.

Common wall A wall separating two units in a condominium, duplex, or other multi-unit property.

Community property Property that is acquired by a married couple during the course of their marriage and is considered in many states to be owned jointly, unless certain circumstances are present.

Comparable sales Also called Comps or Comparables. The recent selling prices of similar properties in the area that are used to help determine the market value of a property, with the assumption that the subject property will sell at a similar price to other similar properties.

Comparables Properties used in an appraisal report that are substantially equivalent to the subject property.

Comparative unit method An appraisal technique used to establish specific units of measurement for appraising specific types of property. For example, parking garages are typically compared on a per parking space basis; land is compared per acre or square foot.

Competent party Persons legally capable of entering a contract. Persons who are under age, mentally insane, or under the influence are not competent parties.

Competition The appraisal principle that states that excess profits generate competition.

Competitive Market Analysis (CMA) A comparison of the prices of recently sold homes similar to a listing seller's home in terms of location, style, and amenities. Also known as a comparative market analysis.

Completion bond A legal instrument that guarantees the completion of a project according to specifications.

Component depreciation Component depreciation involves dividing real estate improvements into various components like plumbing, electrical systems, and building shells, and depreciating each component separately for tax purposes. Component depreciation was eliminated by the 1981 Tax Act for any properties purchased after 1980.

Compound interest The amount of interest paid on the principal balance of a mortgage in addition to accrued interest.

Computerized Loan Origination (CLO) An electronic network for handling loan applications through remote computer terminals linked to various lenders' computers.

Concessions Cash, or the equivalent, that the landlord pays or allows in the form of rental abatement, additional tenant finish allowance, moving expenses, or other costs expended in order to persuade a tenant to sign a lease.

Condemnation A government agency's act of taking private property, without the owner's consent, for public use through the power of eminent domain.

Conditional commitment A lender's agreement to make a loan providing the borrower meets certain conditions.

Conditional sale A contract to sell a property which states that the seller will retain the title until all contractual conditions have been fulfilled.

Conditional use permit Written governmental permission allowing a use inconsistent with zoning but necessary for the common good, such as locating an emergency medical facility in a predominantly residential area.

Condominium A type of ownership in which all of the unit owners own the property, common areas, and buildings jointly, and have sole ownership in the unit to which they hold the title.

Condominium conversion Changing an existing rental property's ownership to the condominium form of ownership.

Condominium hotel A condominium project that involves registration desks, short-term occupancy, food and telephone services, and daily cleaning services, and is generally operated as a commercial hotel even though the units are individually owned.

Condominium owners' association An organization of all unit owners that oversees the common elements and enforces the bylaws.

Confession of judgment clause Permits judgment to be entered against a debtor without the creditor having to institute legal proceedings.

Conforming loan A mortgage that meets the conditions to be purchased by Fannie Mae or Freddie Mac.

Conformity The appraisal principle that holds that the greater the similarity among properties in an area, the better they will hold their value. In general, conformity assumes that a neighborhood that is reasonably similar in social and economic activity will result in properties that reach their maximum value.

Conservator A person appointed by the court to administer the personal affairs or property of an individual who is not capable of handling those duties.

Consideration That received by the grantor in exchange for his or her deed; something of value that induces a person to enter into a contract.

Construction documents The drawings and specifications an architect and/or engineer provides to describe construction requirements for a project.

Construction loan A short-term loan to finance the cost of construction, usually dispensed in stages throughout the construction project. Most construction loans provide for periodic payouts as stages of construction completion are reached.

Construction management The process of ensuring that the stages of the construction project are completed in a timely and seamless manner.

Construction to permanent loan A construction loan that can be converted to a longer-term traditional mortgage after construction is complete. Some construction loans are not convertible, requiring the borrower to obtain separate permanent financing; construction to permanent loans contain provisions allowing the conversion of a construction loan into a conventional mortgage.

Constructive eviction Actions of a landlord that so materially disturb or impair a tenant's enjoyment of the leased premises that the tenant is effectively forced to move out and terminate the lease without liability for any further rent.

Constructive notice Notice given by recorded documents. All people are charged with knowledge of such documents and their contents, whether or not they have actually examined them. Possession of property is also considered constructive notice that the person in possession has an interest in the property.

Consultant An individual or company that provides the services to institutional investors, such as defining real estate investment policies, making recommendations to advisors or managers, analyzing existing real estate portfolios, monitoring and reporting on portfolio performance, and/or reviewing specified investment opportunities.

Consumer Price Index (CPI) A measurement of inflation, relating to the change in the prices of goods and services that are regularly purchased by a specific population during a certain period of time.

Contiguous space Refers to several suites or spaces on a floor (or connected floors) in a given building that can be combined and rented to a single tenant.

Contingency A provision or provisions in a contract that must be met for the contract to be considered enforceable. For example, a buyer may offer a contract that is contingent upon the buyer's obtaining suitable financing; if financing is not obtained, the buyer may back out of the agreement without penalty.

Contingency listing A type of listing that has unusual provisions. For instance, a real estate agent may accept a listing that has an unusually short time frame.

Continuous operation clause Provision in a shopping center lease that requires a store to maintain minimum inventory levels, or more commonly, to remain open during certain hours.

Contour map A map that displays the topography of the site. The map contains contour lines showing various elevations on the site.

Contract A legally enforceable promise or set of promises that must be performed and for which, if a breach of the promise occurs, the law provides a remedy. A contract may be either unilateral, by which only one party is bound to act, or bilateral, by which all parties to the instrument are legally bound to act as prescribed.

Contract for deed An agreement to sell real estate by installment. The buyer may use, occupy, and enjoy the land, but no deed is given until all or a specified part of the sale price has been paid, usually in installments (monthly payments).

Contract for sale A legal document the buyer and seller must approve and sign that details the price and terms of the transaction.

Contract rent Also known as Face Rent. Contract rent is the dollar amount of the rental obligation specified in the lease.

Contractor A person or company who contracts to supply goods or services, generally in connection with the development of a property.

Contribution A principle of valuation that states that the value of any portion of a property is determined by how it affects the performance of the total property. A property is considered to be a combination of features, each of which adds something to the total value based on its contribution to the property.

Controlled business arrangement An arrangement where a package of services (such as a real estate firm, title insurance company, mortgage broker and home inspection company), is offered to consumers.

Conventional loan A long-term loan from a nongovernmental lender that a borrower obtains for the purchase of a home. VA and FHA loans are not considered conventional loans. Fixed rate, fixed term mortgages are typically considered conventional loans.

Conversion Changing property to a different use or form of ownership. For example, an apartment building can be converted to condominiums, or a large residence can be converted to a multi-tenant apartment building.

Convertible Adjustable Rate Mortgage A type of mortgage that begins as a traditional ARM but contains a provision to enable the borrower to change to a fixed-rate mortgage during a certain period of time. Does not require refinancing of the loan.

Convertible debt A mortgage position that gives the lender the option to convert to a partial or full ownership position in a property within a specified time period.

Convertible preferred stock Preferred stock that can be converted to common stock under certain conditions which have been specified by the issuer.

Conveyance A term used to refer to any document that transfers title to real property. The term is also used in describing the act of transferring.

Cooling-off period A grace period provided by law that allows a party to back out of a contract legally within a specified period of time. The Truth in Lending Act requires a cooling off period in transactions involving a personal residence.

Cooperative Also called a co-op. Cooperatives are a type of ownership by multiple residents of a multi-unit housing complex, in which they all own shares in the cooperative corporation that owns the property and have the right to occupy a particular apartment or unit.

Cooperative mortgage Any loan that is related to a cooperative residential project.

Co-ownership Title ownership held by two or more persons.

Core properties The main types of property, specifically office, retail, industrial, and multi-family.

Corporation A legal entity properly registered with the secretary of state. A corporation can have limited liability, perpetual life, freely transferable shares, and centralized management.

Corporeal property Visible or tangible real or personal property. Buildings, fences, sidewalks, and driveways are corporeal property. Easements, for example, are incorporeal.

Co-signer A second individual or party who also signs a promissory note or loan agreement, thereby taking responsibility for the debt in the event that the primary borrower cannot pay. A co-signer typically does not appear on the title or deed.

Cost approach appraisal The process of estimating the value of a property by adding to the estimated land value the appraiser's estimate of the reproduction or replacement cost of the building, less depreciation. The cost approach bases the value of a property on the cost of replacing it, not on the value of other homes in the area or on its ability to generate income.

Cost approach improvement value The current expenses for constructing a copy or replacement for an existing structure, but subtracting an estimate of the accrued depreciation.

Cost approach land value The estimated value of the basic interest in the land if it were available for development to its highest and best use.

Cost of Funds Index (COFI) An index used to determine changes in the interest rates for certain ARMs.

Cost of living index An indicator of the current price level for goods and services related to a base year. Reflects the increase or decrease in the cost of certain commodities and services.

Cost recovery An Internal Revenue Service term for depreciation.

Cost-of-sale percentage An estimate of the expenses of selling an investment that represents brokerage commissions, closing costs, fees, and other necessary sales costs.

Costs plus contract An agreement on a construction project where the contractor is provided a specified profit over and above the actual costs of construction. Most homeowners avoid these contracts because the contractor has little incentive to keep costs down.

Counteroffer A new offer made in response to an offer received. It has the effect of rejecting the original offer, which cannot be accepted thereafter unless revived by the offerer.

Coupon The token or expected interest rate the borrower is charged on a promissory note or mortgage.

Courier fee The fee that is charged at closing for the delivery of documents between all parties concerned in a real estate transaction.

Courtesy to brokers The practice of sharing commissions between listing and cooperating brokers.

Covenant A written agreement between two or more parties in which a party or parties pledge to perform or not perform specified acts with regard to property; usually found in such real estate documents as deeds, mortgages, leases, and contracts for deed.

Covenant not to complete A clause in an agreement where a party promises not to sell or produce the same goods and services within a specified geographic area of the other party. Also known as a non-compete clause or covenant.

Covenant of quiet enjoyment The covenant implied by law by which a landlord guarantees that a tenant may take possession of leased premises and that the landlord will not interfere in the tenant's possession or use of the property.

Creative financing Any financing arrangement other than a traditional mortgage from a third-party lending institution. Creative financing can include loans from the seller, balloon payment loans, wraparound mortgages, and land contracts.

Credit An agreement in which a borrower promises to repay the lender at a later date and receives something of value in exchange.

Credit enhancement The necessary credit support, in addition to mortgage collateral, in order to achieve the desired credit rating on mortgage-backed securities.

Credit history An individual's record which details his or her current and past financial obligations and performance.

Credit life insurance A type of insurance that pays the balance of a mortgage if the borrower dies.

Credit rating The degree of creditworthiness a person is assigned based on his credit history and current financial status.

Credit report An individual's record detailing an individual's credit, employment, and residence history used to determine the individual's creditworthiness.

Credit repository A company that records and updates credit applicants' financial and credit information from various sources.

Credit score Sometimes called a Credit Risk Score. A credit score is the number listed on a consumer credit report that represents a statistical summary of the information.

Creditor A party to whom other parties owe money.

Cross collateralization A group of mortgages or properties that jointly secures one debt obligation.

Cross defaulting A provision that allows a trustee or lender to require full payment on all loans in a group, if any single loan in the group is in default.

Cumulative discount rate A percentage of the current value of base rent with all landlord lease concessions taken into account.

Curable depreciation Depreciation or deterioration that can be corrected at a cost less than the value that will be added. For example, if a house in poor condition can be rehabbed for a cost of $30,000 that will result in an added value of $50,000, the depreciation is considered curable.

Curb appeal The attractiveness of a house or property as viewed from the street.

Current occupancy The current percentage of units in a building or property that is leased.

Current yield The amount of the coupon divided by the price.

Curtsey The right of a husband to all or part of his deceased wife's realty regardless of the provisions of her will. Curtsey only exists in a few states.

Customer The third party for whom some level of service is provided.

Damages The amount recoverable by a person who has been injured in any manner, including physical harm, property damage, or violated rights, through the act or default of another. For example, a landlord whose apartment has been damaged by a tenant will seek monetary damages.

Datum A horizontal plane from which heights and depths are measured.

DBA Stands for Doing Business As; is used to identify a trade name or a fictitious business name. A company using the designation DBA is not attempting to mislead or defraud customers.

Deal structure The type of agreement reached in financing an acquisition. The deal can be unleveraged, leveraged, traditional debt, participating debt, participating/convertible debt, or a joint venture.

Debasement A right to use the land of another for a specific purpose, such as for a right-of-way or utilities.

Debenture An unsecured note or bond. A debenture, unlike a mortgage, does not have an underlying asset which serves as security for the debt.

Debt Any amount one party owes to another party; an obligation to pay.

Debt coverage ratio The relationship between net operating income and annual debt service. The debt coverage ratio is often used as a way to evaluate an income property's suitability for loan approval.

Debt service The amount of money that is necessary to meet all interest and principal payments on a loan during a specific period.

Debt Service Coverage Ratio (DSCR) A property's yearly net operating income divided by the yearly cost of debt service.

Debt-to-equity ratio The relationship between the level of debt and the level of equity in a property. For example, a property with a mortgage of $100,000 and equity of $25,000 has a debt-to-equity ratio of 4:1.

Debt-to-income ratio The percentage of a borrower's monthly payment on long-term debts divided by his gross monthly income.

Debtor The person obligated to pay a debt. The debtor is the opposite of a creditor.

Decedent A person who has died.

Declaration Formal pleadings made by a plaintiff as to the facts that caused his or her actions. A declaration is also a statement made out of court.

Declaration of restrictions The set of restrictions filed by a subdivision or a condominium listing rules residents must follow.

Declining balance method A method of depreciation where a rate is applied to the remaining balance to determine the depreciation deduction.

Decree An order by a person in authority; usually from a court or government agency.

Dedication The voluntary transfer of private property by its owner to the public for some public use, such as for streets or schools.

Deed A legal document that conveys property ownership to the buyer. The seller delivers a deed to the buyer after the transaction (including the exchange of funds) has been completed.

Deed in lieu of foreclosure The act of giving a property back to the lender without undergoing foreclosure. While the end result is the same—the lender regains possession of the property—the expense and repercussions of the foreclosure proceedings is avoided.

Deed in trust An instrument that grants a trustee under a land trust full power to sell, mortgage, and subdivide a parcel of real estate. The beneficiary controls the trustee's use of these powers under the provisions of the trust agreement. A provision that allows a lender to foreclose on a property in the event that the borrower defaults on the loan.

Deed of trust An instrument used in some states instead of a mortgage. Legal title to the property is vested in one or more trustees to secure the repayment of a loan. The deed of trust allows the lender to regain possession in case of default.

Deed restrictions Clauses in a deed limiting the future uses of the property. Deed restrictions may impose a vast variety of limitations and conditions; for example, they may limit the density of buildings, dictate the types of structures that can be erected, or prevent buildings from being used for specific purposes or even from being used at all.

Default The state that occurs when a borrower fails to fulfill a duty or take care of an obligation, such as making monthly mortgage payments. Not fulfilling conditions of a contract causes the party to be in default.

Default judgment A court order in favor of the plaintiff that results from the defendant's failure to appear in court or to answer the original complaint.

Defeasance clause A clause used in leases and mortgages that cancels a specified right upon the occurrence of a certain condition, such as the termination of a mortgage once a mortgage loan is repaid.

Defendant The part sued in an action at law. If one party sues another, the party bringing suit (filing the complaint) is the plaintiff; the party who has been brought suit against is the defendant.

Deferred maintenance A lack of normal upkeep. Deferred maintenance is an appraisal term used to note items like broken windows, missing shingles, peeling paint, broken guttering, and other property defects that have not been addressed by the owner.

Deferred Maintenance Account (DMA) A type of account that a borrower must fund to provide for maintenance of a property.

Deferred payment method The system of making payments at a later date. For example, on a graduated payment mortgage the principal payments and some interest payments are deferred for the first two to five years.

Deficiency judgment A personal judgment levied against the borrower when a foreclosure sale does not produce sufficient funds to pay the mortgage debt in full.

Defined Benefit Plan (DBP) A type of benefit provided by an employer that defines an employee's benefits either as a fixed amount or a percentage of the beneficiary's salary when he retires.

Defined Contribution Plan (DCP) A type of benefit plan provided by an employer in which an employee's retirement benefits are determined by the amount that has been contributed by the employer and/or employee during the time of employment, and by the actual investment earnings on those contributions over the life of the fund.

Delayed exchange A transaction where a property is traded for the promise to provide a replacement in-kind property in the near future. By delaying the exchange, the party involved can defer taxable gains on the original property.

Delinquency A state that occurs when the borrower fails to make mortgage payments on time, eventually resulting in foreclosure if payments are chronically late.

Delinquent mortgage A mortgage in which the borrower is behind on payments.

Delivery Transfer of the possession of an item (including real estate) to another person.

Demand The amount of goods people are willing and able to buy at a given price; often coupled with supply.

Demand loan A loan that may be called by the lender at any time; the lender can require repayment of the entire loan balance at any time, for any reason.

Demised premises Property subject to a lease. In a lease, an apartment is referred to as the demised premises.

Demising wall A separation between two tenants, or between a tenant and a hallway or corridor. The demising wall creates a boundary between two apartments, for example.

Density The intensity of land use. For example, if a subdivision has 20 homes in a 20-acre area, the density is one dwelling unit per acre.

Density zoning Zoning ordinances that restrict the maximum average number of houses per acre that may be built within a particular area, generally in a subdivision.

Department of Housing and Urban Development (HUD) Government agency that implements federal housing and community development programs. Attempts to assure decent, safe, and sanitary housing, and investigates complaints of discrimination in housing.

Depletion A deduction to account for reduced land value due to removing minerals.

Deposit Also referred to as Earnest Money. Refers to the funds that the buyer provides when offering to purchase property.

Depreciable real property Real estate that is subject to deductions for depreciation. Generally refers to property used in a business, or as an investment.

Depreciation A decline in the value of property or an asset, often used as a tax deductible item.

Depreciation In appraisal, a loss of value in property due to any cause, including physical deterioration, functional obsolescence, and external obsolescence. In real estate investment, an expense deduction for tax purposes taken over the period of ownership of income property.

Depreciation recapture When real property is sold at a gain and accelerated depreciation has been claimed, the owner may be required to pay a tax at ordinary (non-accelerated) rates to the extent of the excess accelerated depreciation.

Depth tables Percentages applied that indicate the relative value of segments of a property at varying distances from a road. Assumes that property closest to the road has the highest value and farthest from the road has the least value.

Derivative securities A type of securities that has been created from other financial instruments.

Descent Acquisition of an estate by inheritance in which an heir succeeds to the property by operation of law.

Description Formal depiction of the dimensions and locations of a property; serves as the legal location for deed, mortgage, and lease purposes.

Designated agent A licensee who is authorized by a broker to act as an agent for a specific principal in a transaction.

Design-build An approach in which a single individual or business is responsible for both the design and construction of a project.

Developer One who attempts to put land to its most profitable use through the construction of improvements. A person creating a subdivision is a developer.

Development loan Same as a construction loan; monies borrowed to buy land, prepare the site, and construct buildings or dwellings.

Devise The gift of real property by will. The donor (giver) is the devisor and the recipient is the devisee.

Devisee The recipient of real property transferred through the use of a will. The donor is called the devisor.

Devisor The donor of real property transferred through the use of a will. The recipient is called the devisee.

Direct reduction mortgage A loan that requires both interest and principal with each payment so that the level payment will be adequate for amortization over the loan's term. Simply put, the total of all monthly mortgage payments will fulfill the terms of the loan.

Direct sales comparisons approach Same as a market comparison approach; an appraisal approach where value is estimated by analyzing sales prices of similar properties recently sold.

Disbursement Paying out money, such as when a loan is originated or when a business or investment is concluded. Monies given to the borrower at a closing are disbursements.

Discharge in bankruptcy The release of a bankrupt party from the obligation to repay debts that were proved in a bankruptcy proceeding.

Disclaimer A statement where responsibility is rejected, or to give up ownership of property.

Disclosure A written statement, presented to a potential buyer, that lists information relevant to a piece of property, whether positive or negative.

Discount The difference between the face amount of an obligation and the amount given or received.

Discount broker A broker who provides service for a lower commission than what is typical in the market. Many discount brokers also charge flat fees rather than on a percentage basis.

Discount point A unit of measurement used to describe various loan charges; one point equals 1 percent of the amount of the loan. For example, $2,000 equals one discount point on a $200,000 loan. Typically discount points are fees that a lender charges to provide a lower interest rate.

Discretion The amount of authority an adviser or manager is granted for investing and managing a client's capital.

Discrimination Applying special treatment — typically unfavorable — to an individual due to the individual's race, religion, or sex.

Disintermediation A situation where deposits are removed from a financial intermediary, like a bank, and invested in other assets in order to obtain higher yields.

Dispossess proceedings The legal process where a landlord removes a tenant and regains possession of a property. Also used to describe the process of eviction.

Distraint The legal right of a landlord to seize a tenant's personal property to satisfy payment of back rent.

Diversification The act of spreading individual investments out to insulate a portfolio against the risk of reduced yield or capital loss.

Dividend Distributions of cash or stock that stockholders receive.

Dividend yield The percentage of a security's market price that represents the annual dividend rate.

Document needs list The list of documents a lender requires from a potential borrower who is submitting a loan application.

Documentation preparation fee A fee that lenders, brokers, and/or settlement agents charge for the preparation of the necessary closing documents.

Documents Written or printed papers.

Dollar stop An agreed amount of taxes and operating expenses each tenant must pay out on a prorated basis.

Domicile The place in which an individual makes his or her primary residence.

Dominant tenement A property that includes in its ownership the appurtenant right to use an easement over another person's property for a specific purpose.

Double taxation Taxation of the same income at two levels. For example, a corporation could pay taxes on corporate income, then distribute dividends to shareholders who pay taxes on the dividend income. This situation is considered double taxation.

Dower The legal right or interest, recognized in some states, that a wife acquires in the property her husband held or acquired during their marriage. During the husband's lifetime the right is only a possibility of an interest; upon his death it can become an interest in land.

Down payment The difference between the purchase price and the portion that the mortgage lender financed. A down payment typically refers to the amount of cash a borrower puts down on the house.

Downzoning The act of rezoning a tract of land for a less intensive use than the existing or permitted use. For example, land zoned for industrial purposes could be downzoned to residential use.

Draw A payment from the construction loan proceeds made to contractors, subcontractors, home builders, or suppliers.

Dry closing A closing that is complete except for disbursing funds and delivering documents. The parties in the closing have fulfilled their duties, and the escrow must complete the closing.

Dry mortgage A mortgage that carries no personal liability for the borrower; the lender may take the property pledged as collateral for the loan, but have no recourse to other assets of the borrower. Also called a non-recourse loan.

Dual agency An individual or company representing both parties to a transaction. Dual agencies are unethical unless both parties agree, and are illegal in many states.

Due diligence The activities of a prospective purchaser or mortgagor of real property for the purpose of confirming that the property is as represented by the seller and is not subject to environmental or other problems. A person performing due diligence is making a reasonable effort to perform under a contract, is making a reasonable effort to provide accurate and complete information, and/or is examining a property to detect the presence of contaminants or defects.

Due on sale clause A provision in the mortgage that states that the entire balance of the note is immediately due and payable if the mortgagor transfers (sells) the property.

Duplex Two dwellings under the same roof.

Duress Unlawful constraint or action exercised upon a person whereby the person is forced to perform an act against his or her will; a compulsion to do something because of a threat. A contract entered into under duress is voidable.

Dwelling A place of residence.

Early occupancy Allowing a buyer to take possession of a property before closing.

Earnest money Money deposited by a buyer under the terms of a contract, to be forfeited if the buyer defaults but applied to the purchase price if the sale is closed.

Earthquake insurance A type of insurance policy that provides coverage against earthquake damage to a home.

Easement The right given to a non-ownership party to use a certain part of the property for specified purposes, such as servicing power lines or cable lines.

Easement by condemnation An easement created by the government or government agency that has exercised its right under eminent domain.

Easement by necessity An easement allowed by law as necessary for the full enjoyment of a parcel of real estate; for example, a right of ingress and egress over a grantor's land.

Easement by prescription An easement acquired by continuous, open, and hostile use of the property for the period of time prescribed by state law.

Easement in gross An easement that is not created for the benefit of any land owned by the owner of the easement but that attaches personally to the easement owner. For example, a right granted by Joan Smith to John Baker to use a portion of her property for the rest of his life would be an easement in gross.

Economic feasibility The viability of a building or project in terms of costs and revenue where the degree of viability is established by extra revenue.

Economic life The number of years during which an improvement will add value to the land.

Economic obsolescence Losses of value from causes outside the property itself. Also referred to as environmental obsolescence and external obsolescence. For example, the value of a home could drop if a large apartment building is constructed on the next lot.

Economic rent The market rental value of a property at a particular point in time.

Effective gross income The potential gross income of an income property, minus a vacancy and collection allowance.

Effective age An estimate of the physical condition of a building presented by an appraiser.

Effective date The date on which the sale of securities can commence once a registration statement becomes effective.

Effective Gross Income (EGI) The total property income which rents and other sources generate after subtracting a vacancy factor estimated to be appropriate for the property.

Effective Gross Rent (EGR) The net rent that is generated after adjusting for tenant improvements and other capital costs, lease commissions and other sales expenses.

Effective interest rate The true rate of return considering all relevant financing expenses.

Effective rent The actual rental rate that the landlord achieves after deducting the concession value from the base rental rate a tenant pays.

Efficiency unit A small dwelling, usually consisting of a single room, within a multi-family structure. In many cases kitchen or bath facilities are not complete. For example, an efficiency apartment may have a microwave and sink, but no stove or refrigerator.

Egress Access from land to a public road or other means of exit.

Ejectment An action to regain possession of real property when there is no lease.

Electronic authentication A way of providing proof that a particular electronic document is genuine, has arrived unaltered, and came from the indicated source.

Elevation drawing A non-perspective drawing of a property from the front, rear, or side that indicates how the planned or existing structure is situated.

Ellwood technique Appraisal of income property designed to estimate the present value of the property. Evaluates cash flow, resale proceeds, and the capitalization rate to determine value.

Emblement A growing crop. Crops that grow annually are typically considered personal property.

Eminent domain The power of the government to pay the fair market value for a property, appropriating it for public use.

Employee Someone who works for an employer and has employee status. The employer is obligated to withhold income taxes and Social Security taxes from the compensation of employees. An independent contractor is not an employee.

Employee Retirement Income Security Act (ERISA) Legislation that controls the investment activities, mainly of corporate and union pension plans.

Employment contract A document indicating formal employment between employer and employee or between principal and agent. In the real estate business an employment contract generally takes the form of a listing agreement or management agreement.

Empty nester Couples whose children have established separate households.

Encapsulation A method of controlling environmental contamination by sealing off a dangerous substance.

Encroachment A building or some portion of it—a wall or fence for instance—that extends beyond the land of the owner and illegally intrudes on some land of an adjoining owner or a street or alley. Any improvement or upgrade that illegally intrudes onto another party's property.

Encumbrance Anything—such as a mortgage, tax, or judgment lien, an easement, a restriction on the use of the land or an outstanding dower right—that may diminish the value or use and enjoyment of a property.

End loan The result of converting to permanent financing from a construction loan. A conventional mortgage is an end loan.

Endorsement The act of signing one's name, as the payee, on the back of a check or note; offering support or credibility to a statement.

Enjoin To forbid or command the performance of an act. For example, a homeowner can ask the court to enjoin a neighbor to clean up his property if it is in an unhealthy state.

Enrolled agent A tax professional licensed by the government to deal with the Internal Revenue Service on behalf of consumers.

Entitlement To be owed something under the law; the portion of a VA loan that protects the lender if the veteran defaults.

Entity A person or corporation that is recognized by law.

Entrepreneur An individual who generates business activity; a businessperson; a person who takes business risks.

Environmental audit A study of the property to determine whether there are any hazards.

Environmental Impact Statement Legally required documents that must accompany major project proposals where there will likely be an impact on the surrounding environment.

Environmental Protection Agency (EPA) The agency of the United States government that enforces federal pollution laws and implements pollution prevention programs.

Epitome An abstract of title in book form.

Equal Credit Opportunity Act (ECOA) A federal law that requires a lender or other creditor to make credit available for applicants regardless of sex, marital status, race, religion, or age.

Equalization The raising or lowering of assessed values for tax purposes in a particular county or taxing district to make them equal to assessments in other counties or districts.

Equalization board A government agency that determines the fairness of taxes levied against properties.

Equalization factor A factor (number) by which the assessed value of a property is multiplied to arrive at a value for the property that is in line with statewide tax assessments. The ad valorem tax would be based on this adjusted value.

Equifax One of the three primary credit-reporting bureaus.

Equitable conversion A legal doctrine used in some states where, under a contract of sale, buyers and sellers are treated as though the closing had taken place in that the seller has an obligation to take care of the property.

Equitable lien A legal document that encumbers the property but is not technically a mortgage because of the existence of some legal error.

Equitable right of redemption The right of a defaulted property owner to recover the property prior to its sale by paying the appropriate fees and charges.

Equitable title The interest held by a vendee under a contract for deed or an installment contract; the equitable right to obtain absolute ownership to property when legal title is held in another's name.

Equity The value of a property after existing liabilities have been deducted; the value of a property over and above all liens against it. A property worth $400,000 with loans totaling $300,000 against it has an equity of $100,000.

Equity buildup The gradual increase in equity due to the gradual payoff of the loan principal through monthly payments.

Equity mortgage A line of credit offered against the equity in a home. The equity is secured by a second mortgage on the home. Also called a home equity loan.

Equity of redemption The right of an owner to reclaim property before a foreclosure sale. If the owner can raise enough funds to pay principal, interest, and taxes on the property, he can reclaim the property before a foreclosure sale, even though foreclosure proceedings may be under way.

Equity sharing loan A loan where a resident-owner splits equity increases in the value of the home with an investor-owner who contributes towards the down payment and monthly payments of the home.

Erosion The gradual wearing away of land by water, wind, and general weather conditions; the diminishing of property by the elements.

Errors and Omissions Insurance A type of policy that insures against the mistakes of a builder or architect.

Escalation clause The clause in a lease that provides for the rent to be increased to account for increases in the expenses the landlord must pay.

Escalator clause A provision in a lease that requires the tenant to pay more rent based on an increase in costs.

Escape clause A provision in a contract that allows one or more of the parties to cancel all or part of the contract if certain events do not occur. For example, a buyer who cannot get approval for financing can cancel the contract if an appropriate escape clause is included in the contract for sale.

Escheat The reversion of property to the state or county, as provided by state law, in cases where a decedent dies intestate without heirs capable of inheriting, or when the property is abandoned.

Escrow The closing of a transaction through a third party called an escrow agent who receives certain funds and documents to be delivered upon the performance of certain conditions outlined in the escrow instructions. A valuable item, money or documents deposited with a third party for delivery upon the fulfillment of a condition.

Escrow account Also referred to as an Impound Account. An account established by a mortgage lender or servicing company for the purpose of holding funds for the payment of items, such as homeowners insurance and property taxes.

Escrow agent A neutral third party who makes sure that all conditions of a real estate transaction have been met before any funds are transferred or property is recorded.

Escrow agreement A written agreement between an escrow agent and the contractual parties which defines the basic obligations of each party, the money (or other valuables) to be deposited in escrow, and how the escrow agent is to dispose of the money on deposit.

Escrow analysis An annual investigation a lender performs to make sure they are collecting the appropriate amount of money for anticipated expenditures.

Escrow closing The event in which all conditions of a real estate transaction have been met, and the property title is transferred to the buyer.

Escrow company A neutral company that serves as a third party to ensure that all conditions of a real estate transaction are met.

Escrow contract An agreement between a buyer, seller, and escrow holder setting forth rights and responsibilities of each. An escrow contract is entered into when earnest money is deposited in a broker's escrow account.

Escrow disbursements The dispensing of escrow funds for the payment of real estate taxes, hazard insurance, mortgage insurance, and other property expenses as they are due.

Escrow instructions A document that sets forth the duties of the escrow agent, as well as the requirements and obligations of the parties, when a transaction is closed through an escrow.

Escrow payment The funds that are withdrawn by a mortgage servicer from a borrower's escrow account to pay property taxes and insurance.

Estate The total assets, including property, of an individual after he has died.

Estate at sufferance The tenancy of a lessee who lawfully comes into possession of a landlord's real estate but who continues to occupy the premises improperly after his or her lease rights have expired.

Estate at will An estate that gives the lessee the right to possession until the estate is terminated by either party; the term of this estate is indefinite.

Estate at will The occupation of real estate by a tenant for an indefinite period, terminable by one or both parties at will. The landlord may evict the tenant at any time, and the tenant may vacate the property at any time.

Estate for years An interest for a certain exact period of time in property leased for a specified consideration.

Estate from period to period An interest in leased property that continues from period to period — week to week, month to month, or year to year.

Estate in land The degree, quantity, nature, and extent of interest a person has in real property.

Estate taxes Federal taxes on a decedent's real and personal property.

Estimated closing costs An estimation of the expenses relating to the sale of real estate.

Estimated hazard insurance An estimation of hazard insurance, or homeowners' insurance, that will cover physical risks.

Estimated property taxes An estimation of the property taxes that must be paid on the property, according to state and county tax rates.

Estoppel A doctrine of law that stops a person from later denying facts which the person once acknowledged as true, and that others took to be true in good faith. A person who signs a contract stating he will pay $10,000 cannot later argue he only owes $5,000 under estoppel.

Estoppel Certificate A signed statement that certifies that certain factual statements are correct as of the date of the statement and can be relied upon by a third party, such as a prospective lender or purchaser.

Estovers The legally supported right to take necessities from a property. A person with a life estate on a property could, for example, cut trees to use for firewood.

Et al. Abbreviation that means "and others."

Et ux. Abbreviation that means "and wife."

Et vir. Abbreviation that means "and husband."

Ethics The system of moral principles and rules that become standards for professional conduct.

Ethnic group People belonging to the same race, or having a common heritage of language, culture, or customs.

Eviction The legal removal of an occupant from a piece of property.

Evidence of title Proof of ownership of property; commonly a certificate of title, an abstract of title with lawyer's opinion, title insurance, or a Torrens registration certificate.

Examination of title A title company's inspection and report of public records and other documents for the purpose of determining the chain of ownership of a property.

Exception An item not covered by an insurance policy.

Excess condemnation The taking of more land than is actually used to meet the public purpose of the condemnation under eminent domain. Excess condemnation land is often sold at auction at a later date.

Exchange A transaction in which all or part of the consideration is the transfer of like-kind property (such as real estate for real estate).

Exclusionary zoning Zoning laws of a community that serve to prohibit low and moderate income housing. Exclusionary zoning is considered illegal.

Exclusive agency listing A listing contract under which the owner appoints a real estate broker as his or her exclusive agent for a designated period of time to sell the property, on the owner's stated terms, for a commission. The owner reserves the right to sell without paying anyone a commission if he or she sells to a prospect that has not been introduced or claimed by the broker.

Exclusive agency listing A written agreement between a property owner and a real estate broker in which the owner promises to pay the broker a commission if certain property is leased during the listing period.

Exclusive listing A contract that allows a licensed real estate agent to be the only agent who can sell a property for a given time.

Exclusive right to sell An employment contract giving the broker the right to collect a commission on the sale of the property by any party, including the owner, during the terms of the agreement.

Exclusive right to sell listing A listing contract under which the owner appoints a real estate broker as his or her exclusive agent for a designated period of time, to sell the property on the owner's stated terms, and agrees to pay the broker a commission when the property is sold, whether by the broker, the owner, or another broker.

Exculpatory clause A provision in a mortgage allowing the borrower to surrender the property to the lender without personal liability for the loan.

Execute To sign a contract; to perform a contract fully.

Executed contract An agreement in which all parties involved have fulfilled their duties.

Execution The signing and delivery of an instrument. Also, execution is a legal order directing an official to enforce a judgment against the property of a debtor.

Executor The individual who is named in a will to administer an estate. "Executrix" is the feminine form.

Executory contract A contract under which something remains to be done by one or more of the parties.

Exhibit A document presented as supporting data for principal document. For example, a contract may have a legal description of the property attached.

Exit strategy An approach investors may use when they wish to liquidate all or part of their investment.

Expansion option A provision in a lease granting a tenant the option to lease additional adjacent space after a specified period of time; common in commercial leases.

Expense stop A dollar limit above which the tenant in a commercial lease agrees to pay operating expenses. Serves as a protection for the landlord against unforeseen increases in operating expenses.

Experian One of the three primary credit-reporting bureaus.

Exposure The amount a person or company could lose in an investment; the advertising of property that is for sale.

Express agency An agency relationship based on a formal agreement between the parties.

Express agreement An oral or written contract in which the parties state the contract's terms and express their intentions in words.

Expropriation Seizure of private property for public use by an entity with the legal authority to do so. Similar to condemnation through eminent domain.

Extended coverage Insurance that covers specific incidences normally not covered by standard homeowners policies. For example, a homeowner who lives next to a baseball field may obtain extended coverage to insure against window damage from balls.

Extender clause A condition providing for a listing agreement to be automatically renewable until the parties agree to terminate it. Rarely used at present.

Extension An agreement between two parties to extend the time period specified in a contract. Both parties must agree.

External depreciation Reduction in a property's value caused by outside factors (those that are off the property).

External obsolescence Incurable depreciation caused by factors not on subject property, such as environmental, social, or economic factors.

Façade The outside front wall of a building or structure.

Face rental rate The rent rate that the landlord publishes.

Face value The dollar amount on a document.

Facility space The floor area in a hospitality property that is dedicated to activities, such as restaurants, health clubs, and gift shops that interactively service multiple people and is not directly related to room occupancy.

FAD multiple The price per share of a REIT divided by its funds available for distribution

Fair Credit Reporting Act (FCRA) The federal legislation that governs the processes credit reporting agencies must follow.

Fair Housing Act The federal law that prohibits discrimination in housing based on race, color, religion, sex, handicap, familial status, and national origin.

Fair market value The highest price that a buyer would be willing to pay, and the lowest a seller would be willing to accept.

False advertising Describing property in a misleading fashion.

Familial status Defined by the Fair Housing Act; a characteristic determined by a person's household where one or more individuals under the age of 18 live with a parent or legal guardian. Prohibits denying rights to people under the age of 18 who live with a parent or guardian.

Fannie Mae Federal National Mortgage Association. A quasi-government agency established to purchase any kind of mortgage loans in the secondary mortgage market from the primary lenders.

Fannie Mae Community Home Buyers Program A community lending model based on borrower income in which mortgage insurers and Fannie Mae offer flexible underwriting guidelines to increase the buying power for a low- or moderate-income family and to decrease the total amount of cash needed to purchase a home.

Farm assets Assets of a farm or ranch including farmland, personal residences, and other structures used in the business of farming or ranching.

Farm Credit System A federal agency of the Department of Agriculture that offers programs to help families purchase or operate family farms.

Farmer Mac Federal Agricultural Mortgage Corporation. An agency that operates similarly to Fannie Mae and Freddie Mac, but for agricultural loans.

Farmer's Home Administration (FMHA) An agency within the U.S. Department of Agriculture that provides credit to farmers and other rural residents.

Farmland Land specifically used for agricultural purposes in the raising of crops or livestock. Land designated in zoning laws for agricultural purposes.

Feasibility study A determination of the likelihood that a proposed development will fulfill the objectives of a particular investor. Typically evaluates expenses, income, and most advantageous use and design.

Federal Deposit Insurance Corporation (FDIC) An independent federal agency that insures the deposits in commercial banks.

Federal Emergency Management Agency (FEMA) Among other duties, offers flood insurance to property owners in designated flood plains.

Federal Home Loan Mortgage Corporation (FHLMC) Also known as Freddie Mac. Buys mortgages from lending institutions, combines them with other loans, and sells shares to investors.

Federal Housing Administration (FHA) A government agency that administers many loan programs, loan guarantee programs, and loan insurance programs designed to make housing more available.

Federal land bank Specialized government-sponsored lenders. Makes loans for land purchase, refinancing, and renovation work on rural real estate.

Federal National Mortgage Association (FNMA) Also known as Fannie Mae. A congressionally chartered, shareholder-owned company that is the nation's largest supplier of home mortgage funds. The company buys mortgages from lenders and resells them as securities on the secondary mortgage market.

Federal Reserve System The country's central banking system, which is responsible for the nation's monetary policy by regulating the supply of money and interest rates.

Federal revenue stamp Stamp that, when affixed to a transaction document, indicates payment of a federal tax imposed on the transaction. Have not been required since 1968.

Federal Savings and Loan Insurance Corporation (FSLIC) Government agency that insures deposits of up to $100,000 in savings and loan associations.

Federal tax lien A debt attached against a property for unpaid federal taxes. Typically used by the Internal Revenue Service to attach property for payment of an owner's unpaid income taxes.

Federal Trade Commission (FTC) Federal agency that regulates advertising and other promotion and sales practices.

Federal underwriters Federal agencies authorized to issue guarantees as credit enhancement for mortgage-backed securities. Includes Fannie Mae, Ginnie Mae, Freddie Mac, and FAMC.

Fee appraiser A professional who furnishes appraisal services for a fee, usually to investors who are considering purchasing property. Also called an independent fee appraiser or a review appraiser.

Fee for service Arrangement where a consumer asks a licensee to perform specific real estate services for a set fee.

Fee simple The highest interest in real estate recognized by the law; the holder is entitled to all rights to the property.

Fee simple absolute The maximum possible estate or right of ownership of real property, continuing forever.

Fee simple determinable A fee simple estate qualified by a special limitation. Language used to describe limitation includes the words, "so long as," or "while," or "during."

Fee simple estate An unconditional, unlimited inheritance estate in which the owner may dispose of or use the property as desired.

Fee simple interest The state of owning all the rights in a real estate parcel.

Feudal system A system of ownership usually associated with pre-colonial England, in which the king or other sovereign is the source of all rights. The right to possess real property was granted by the sovereign to an individual as a life estate only. Upon the death of the individual, title passed back to the sovereign, not to the decedent's heirs.

FFO multiple The price of a REIT share divided by its funds from operations.

FHA loan A loan insured by the Federal Housing Administration and made by an approved lender in accordance with the FHA's regulations.

FHA mortgage insurance A type of insurance that requires a fee to be paid at closing to insure the loan with the Federal Housing Administration (FHA).

Fictitious company name Also called an assumed name; a business name other than that under which the business is registered. Similar to Doing Business As (DBA).

Fidelity bond An assurance, generally purchased by an employer, to cover employees who are entrusted with valuable property or funds.

Fiduciary Any individual who holds authority over a plan's asset management, administration or disposition, or renders paid investment advice regarding a plan's assets.

Fiduciary relationship A relationship of trust and confidence, as between trustee and beneficiary, attorney and client, or principal and agent.

Filled land An area where the grade (level) has been raised by depositing dirt, gravel, or rock. The seller in most cases has the responsibility to disclose filled land to potential buyers.

Finance charge The amount of interest to be paid on a loan or credit card balance.

Finance fee Mortgage brokerage fee to cover the expenses incurred in placing a mortgage with a lending institution.

Financial institution A company in the business of making loans, investments, or obtaining deposits.

Financial statement A document that shows income and expenses for an accounting period, including assets, liabilities, and equity as of a specific point in time.

Financing Borrowing money to buy property or other items. A mortgage is an example of financing.

Financing gap The difference between the selling price of a property and the funds available to the potential homebuyer to purchase the home. A potential buyer who can arrange $80,000 in financing for a home with a sales price of $100,000 is facing a $20,000 financing gap.

Financing statement A document required by the Uniform Commercial Code that establishes a creditor's security interest in personal property.

Fire insurance A form of property insurance covering losses due to fire; often includes additional coverage against smoke or water damage due to a fire.

Fire stop Boards placed between studs or joists to decrease drafts and retard the spread of fire.

Fire wall A wall constructed of fire-resistant materials designed to retard the spread of fire.

Fire yard An area that must be kept clear in order to facilitate the passage of fire vehicles; required by some building codes.

Firm commitment A written agreement a lender makes to loan money for the purchase of property.

First generation space A new space that has never before been occupied by a tenant and is currently available for lease.

First loss position A security's position that will suffer the first economic loss if the assets below it lose value or are foreclosed on.

First mortgage The main mortgage on a property; a mortgage that has priority as a lien before all other mortgages. In the case of foreclosure, the first mortgage will be satisfied before other mortgages.

First papers The initial documentation in a transaction.

Fiscal policy The government's policy in regard to taxation and spending programs. The balance between these two areas determines the amount of money the government will withdraw from or feed into the economy, which can counter economic peaks and slumps.

Fiscal year A continuous 12-month period used for financial reporting; many companies use a fiscal year from January 1st through December 31st.

Fixed costs Expenses remain the same despite the level of sales or production.

Fixed expenses Expenses that remain the same regardless of occupancy. Interest expense is typically considered fixed, while electricity costs are considered to be variable because they typically change from month to month.

Fixed rate An interest rate that does not change over the life of the loan.

Fixed rate loan A loan with an interest rate that does not change over the life of the loan.

Fixed rate mortgage A mortgage with an interest rate that does not change over the length of the mortgage.

Fixed time The particular weeks of a year that the owner of a timeshare arrangement can access his accommodations.

Fixing up expenses Expenses necessary to facilitate a sale; painting, installing new carpet, and landscaping are generally considered fixing up expenses.

Fixture An item of personal property that has been converted to real property by being permanently affixed.

Fixturing period The period during which the lessee enters the premises to make improvements in preparation for opening its business.

Flag lot A method of subdividing land into individual parcels so that compliance with local subdivision regulations can be avoided.

Flat An apartment on one level. A 3-room flat is an apartment that has three rooms on one floor.

Flat fee An amount of money that an adviser or manager receives for managing a portfolio of real estate assets.

Flat lease A rental agreement that requires level (fixed) rent payments.

Flex space A building that provides a flexible configuration of office or showroom space combined with, for example, manufacturing, laboratory, warehouse, distribution.

Flexible payment mortgage A mortgage with payments that are allowed to vary but should be sufficient to allow amortization (payoff) over the mortgage term. Adjustable rate mortgages are flexible payment mortgages.

Flip Purchase and immediately resell property at a quick profit.

Float The number of freely traded shares owned by the public.

Floating lien A loan that will attach to property that is acquired at a later date. Standard loans apply only to property described at the time of the mortgage.

Flood certification The process of analyzing whether a property is located in a known flood zone.

Flood insurance A policy that is required in designated flood zones to protect against loss due to flood damage.

Flood insurance rate map Official maps showing areas that are designated as special flood hazard areas.

Flood prone area An area having a 1 percent annual chance of flooding once every 100 years.

Floodplain Level land subject to periodic flooding from a contiguous body of water. Floodplains are described by the frequency with which flooding is expected; a bi-annual floodplain is expected to be flooded once every two years.

Floor to Area Ratio (FAR) A measurement of a building's gross square footage compared to the square footage of the land on which it is located. Floor to area ratios are often limited by zoning codes.

Floor plan The arrangement of rooms in a building or dwelling.

Flue Chamber in a fireplace that directs smoke and soot through the chimney to the outside.

Flyspecking Careful review of a document—especially an abstract of title, to discover any technical defects.

Footing A concrete support under a foundation that rests in solid ground and is wider than the structure supported. Footings distribute the weight of the structure over the ground.

For Sale By Owner (FSBO) A method of selling property in which the property owner serves as the selling agent and directly handles the sales process with the buyer or buyer's agent.

Forbearance Restraint in taking legal action to remedy a default or other breach of contract in the hope that the default will be cured if additional time is granted.

Force majeure An external force that is not controlled by the contractual parties and prevents them from complying with the provisions of the contract.

Forces and effect of law A phrase referring to the principle that an administrative regulation has the same significance and legal weight as a law or act of legislature.

Foreclosure A legal procedure whereby property used as security for a debt is sold to satisfy the debt in the event of default in payment of the mortgage note or default of other terms in the mortgage document. The foreclosure procedure brings the rights of all parties to a conclusion and passes the title in the mortgaged property to either the holder of the mortgage or a third party who may purchase the realty at the foreclosure sale, free of all encumbrances affecting the property subsequent to the mortgage.

Foreign corporation A corporation established under the laws of anther state or country, and not organized under the state in which it is doing business. A corporation registered in New York doing business in Pennsylvania is considered to be a foreign corporation by entities in Pennsylvania.

Foreshore land Land that is above sea level only at periods of low tide. Because of the tidal action, the land alternates between being wet and dry.

Forfeiture The loss of money or anything of value because of failure to perform a contract.

Forgery The illegal act of counterfeiting documents or making false signatures.

Formica A trade name for a plastic material used primarily for countertops.

Forward commitments Contractual agreements to perform certain financing duties according to any stated conditions.

Foundation drain tile A pipe, usually made of clay, placed next to a foundation to assist water runoff.

Foundation wall The masonry or concrete walls below ground level that serve as the main support for a structure. Foundation walls also form the sides of a basement area.

Four quadrants of the real estate capital markets A phrase referring to the four market types that consist of private equity, public equity, private debt, and public debt.

Fractional section A parcel of land less than 160 acres, usually found at the edge of a rectangular survey.

Franchise An arrangement between a franchisor and a franchisee through which the franchisee uses the company name of the franchisor and is provided specified services in exchange for a fee. Real estate brokerages may operate as franchises of a national company.

Fraud Deception intended to cause a person to give up property or a lawful right.

Freddie Mac Federal Home Loan Mortgage Corporation. Established to purchase primarily conventional mortgage loans in the secondary mortgage market.

Free and clear title Title to a property without encumbrances. Generally used to refer to a title free of mortgage debt. Also known as a clear title or a marketable title.

Free-standing building A structure that is not attached to another structure. A detached garage is considered a free-standing building.

Freehold An interest in real estate without a predetermined time span. A life estate is considered to be a freehold estate because there is no specified time limit to ownership. A lease is not a freehold estate because it has a specified time limit (the length of the lease.)

Freehold estate An estate in land in which ownership is for an indeterminate length of time, in contrast to a leasehold estate.

Front end ratio The measurement a lender uses to compare a borrower's monthly housing expense to gross monthly income.

Front ending Recognition of profits from a transaction before the period during which it is actually earned.

Front footage The measurement of a parcel of land by the number of feet of street or road frontage.

Front money The amount of cash a developer or buyer must have on hand to purchase land and pay other initial expenses before actually developing a project.

Frontage The portion of a lot along a lake, river, street, or highway.

Frontage street A street that is parallel and adjacent to a major street that provides access to abutting properties but is protected from heavy through traffic.

Frost line The depth of frost penetration in the soil; varies according to geographic area and weather conditions. According to building codes, building footings must be placed below the frost line.

Fructus industrials Annual harvestable crops that require cultivation; are generally considered personal property and not real estate. Corn crops are considered fructus industrials.

Fructus naturales Annual harvestable crops that do not require cultivation; are generally classified as real property. Trees are typically classified as personal property.

Full disclosure A requirement to reveal all information pertinent to a transaction. For example, a broker is required under full disclosure to give the buyer all known facts about the physical condition of a property.

Full recourse A loan on which the responsibility of a loan is transferred to an endorser or guarantor in the event of default by the borrower.

Full service rent A rental rate that includes all operating expenses and real estate taxes for the first year.

Fully amortized ARM An ARM with a monthly payment that is sufficient to amortize the remaining balance at the current interest accrual rate over the amortization term.

Fully diluted shares The number of outstanding common stock shares if all convertible securities were converted to common shares.

Functional obsolescence A loss of value to an improvement to real estate arising from functional problems, often caused by age or poor design. For example, a bedroom that can only be entered by walking through another bedroom would be considered functional obsolescence.

Funding fee A fee paid to secure some types of mortgage protection, like the fee paid to the Department of Veterans Affairs for the Veteran's Administration to guarantee a VA loan.

Funds Available for Distribution (FAD) The income from operations, with cash expenditures subtracted, that may be used for leasing commissions and tenant improvement costs.

Funds From Operations (FFO) A ratio that is meant to highlight the amount of cash a company's real estate portfolio generates relative to its total operating cash flow.

Future interest A person's present right to an interest in real property that will not result in possession or enjoyment until some time in the future, such as a reversion or right of reentry.

Future proposed space The space in a commercial development that has been proposed but is not yet under construction, or the future phases of a multi-phase project that has not yet been built.

Gain An increase in money or in property value. A gain is only realized when a property is sold, however.

Gambrel roof A roof with two slopes on two sides; the lower slope is steeper than the upper sections.

Gap A defect in the chain of title of a particular parcel of real estate; a missing document or conveyance that raises doubt as to the present ownership of the land.

Gap group A term used to refer to homebuyers in the moderate income bracket who need some type of assistance or subsidy to qualify for financing.

Gap in title A break in the chain of title; when the records do not reflect a transfer to a particular grantor. Can occur if a grantor fails to record a deed, or when records are otherwise incomplete.

Gap loan A loan that fills the difference between a construction loan and a permanent loan.

Garden apartment A housing complex where some or all tenants have access to a lawn area.

Garnishment A legal process where creditors are repaid for outstanding obligations by attaching a portion of the borrower's paycheck. Garnishments typically can only occur after a judgment occurs.

Gazebo A small, partially enclosed roof structure in a park, garden, or lawn.

General agent An individual or company authorized by a principal to represent the principal.

General contractor The main individual or business responsible for (and contracted to perform) the construction of an entire building or project, rather than individual duties.

General lien The right of a creditor to have all of a debtor's property—real and personal—sold to satisfy a debt.

General partner The member in a partnership who holds the authority to bind the partnership and shares in its profits and losses.

General partnership An organization with only general partners. Each partner is liable beyond the amount invested, and may bind the entire partnership by entering into a contract.

General plan A long-range governmental program to regulate the use and development of property in an orderly fashion; intended to create orderly community growth.

General real estate tax A tax which is made up of the taxes levied on the real estate by government agencies and municipalities.

General Services Administration (GSA) A government agency that manages, leases, and sells buildings owned by the United States government.

General warranty deed A deed in which the grantor fully warrants good clear title to the premises. Used in most real estate deed transfers, a general warranty deed offers the greatest protection of any deed.

Gift Money a buyer has received from a relative or other source.

Gift causa mortis A term used to refer to a gift given in anticipation of death, or to take place only in the event of a death.

Gift deed A deed for which consideration is love and affection, and no material consideration is involved.

Gift letter A letter provided to a lender or government agency acknowledging that money to be used, usually for a down payment, is a gift from a relative or friend and carries no obligation for repayment.

Gift tax Federal tax on a monetary gift to a relative or friend. Currently a person may give up to $11,000 per year to another person without the imposition of federal gift tax.

Ginnie Mae Government National Mortgage Association. A government agency that plays an important role in the secondary mortgage market. It sells mortgage-backed securities that are backed by pools of FHA and VA loans.

Going concern value The entire value of a business, including assets, goodwill with customers, skilled work force, market share, credit lines, and other "assets."

Going in capitalization rate The rate that is computed by dividing the expected net operating income for the first year by the value of the property.

Good consideration A consideration founded on love or affection; usually found in a gift deed. In most cases good consideration is not considered sufficient to form a contract, however.

Good Faith Estimate (GFE) A lender's or broker's estimate that shows all costs associated with obtaining a home loan including loan processing, title, and inspection fees.

Goodwill A business asset of intangible value created by customer and supplier relations. A business with an outstanding reputation may have a higher value due to goodwill.

Government check The 24-mile-square parcels composed of 16 townships in the rectangular (government) survey system of legal description.

Government forces An appraisal factor used to evaluate government controls and regulations, public services, zoning requirements, and building codes. Government forces play a part in determining a property's value.

Government loan A mortgage that is insured or guaranteed by the FHA, the Department of Veterans Affairs (VA), or the Rural Housing Service (RHS).

Government lot Fractional sections in the rectangular (government) survey system less than one quarter-section in area.

Government National Mortgage Association (GNMA) Also known as Ginnie Mae. A government-owned corporation under the U.S. Department of Housing and Urban Development (HUD) which performs the same role as Fannie Mae and Freddie Mac in providing funds to lenders for making home loans, but only purchases loans that are backed by the federal government.

Government patent The original United States land grant that conveyed ownership of government-owned land to the people.

Government survey method The system of land description that applies to most of the land in the United States, particularly land in the western half of the United States.

Grace period A defined time period in which a borrower may make a loan payment after its due date without incurring a penalty.

Grade The elevation of a hill, road, sidewalk, or slope showing its inclination from level ground. Usually expressed as a percentage of level distance: a 10 percent grade rises 10 feet in each 100 feet of level distance.

Gradient The rate of increase or decrease in elevation of a surface, road, or pipe.

Graduated lease A lease, usually long-term, in which rent payments vary in accordance with future specified contingencies.

Graduated payment mortgage (GPM) A loan in which the monthly principal and interest payments increase by a certain percentage each year for a certain number of years and then level off for the remaining loan term.

Graduated rental lease A lease in which rent payments begin at a fixed low rate but increase at established intervals through the term of the lease. Graduated rental leases are often used to entice potential tenants.

Grandfather clause A term used to describe the concept that a previously permissible condition is still permissible despite changes in law or requirements. A structure built prior to building codes may not have to be upgraded; it is considered to be grandfathered in.

Granny flats A small room rented within in a residence that is zoned single-family; also sometimes called in-law apartments.

Grant The term used to indicate a transfer of property. A person can grant property to another person in a deed.

Grant deed A type of deed where the grantor affirms that they have not previously conveyed the property to another person, and the property is not encumbered except as already noted on the deed. Grant deeds are common in California.

Grantee A person who receives a conveyance of real property from a grantor.

Granting clause Words in a deed of conveyance that state the grantor's intention to convey the property at the present time. This clause is generally worded as "convey and warrant," "grant," "grant, bargain, and sell."

Grantor The person transferring title to or an interest in real property to a grantee.

Grantor to grantee index A public record that cross-indexes grantors and grantees to one another, noting the properties they relate to.

Gratuitous agent An agent who receives no compensation for his or her services.

GRI Stands for Graduate, Realtors® Institute. Denotes a person who has completed prescribed courses in law, finance, investment, appraisal, and salesmanship.

Grievance period A specified period of time during which the public may register complaints about tax assessments or other property problems.

Gross area The total floor area of a building, usually measured from the outside walls.

Gross building area The sum of areas at all floor levels, including the basement, mezzanine, and penthouses included in the principal outside faces of the exterior walls without allowing for architectural setbacks or projections.

Gross income The total income of a household before taxes or expenses have been subtracted.

Gross income multiplier A figure used as a multiplier of the gross annual income of a property to produce an estimate of the property's value.

Gross investment in real estate The total amount of equity and debt that is invested in a piece of real estate minus proceeds from sales or partial sales.

Gross leasable area The amount of floor space that is designed for tenants' occupancy and exclusive use.

Gross lease A rental arrangement in which the tenant pays a flat sum for rent, and the landlord must pay all building expenses out of that amount.

Gross real estate asset value The total market value of the real estate investments under management in a fund or individual accounts, usually including the total value of all equity positions, debt positions, and joint venture ownership positions.

Gross real estate investment value The market value of real estate investments that are held in a portfolio without including debt.

Gross Rent Multiplier (GRM) The figure used as a multiplier of the gross monthly income of a property to produce an estimate of the property's value.

Gross returns The investment returns generated from operating a property without adjusting for adviser or manager fees.

Ground area The area of a building computed from the exterior dimensions of the ground floor.

Ground lease A lease of land only, on which the tenant usually owns a building or is required to build as specified in the lease. Such leases are usually long-term net leases; the tenant's rights and obligations continue until the lease expires or is terminated through default.

Ground rent The rent earned by leased land. Also refers to a long-term lease during which rent is paid to the landowner, normally to build something on that land.

Groundwater Water under the surface of the earth.

Growing Equity Mortgage (GEM) A loan in which the monthly payments increase annually, with the increased amount being used to reduce directly the principal balance outstanding and thus shorten the overall term of the loan.

Guaranteed sale program A service offered by some brokers in which they agree to pay the owner of a listed property a predetermined price if the property is not sold within a specified period of time. Because the sale is guaranteed, the owner is free to enter into a contract to purchase another home.

Guarantor The party who makes a guaranty.

Guaranty An agreement in which the guarantor promises to satisfy the debt or obligations of another, if and when the debtor fails to do so.

Guardian An individual appointed by the court to oversee and administer the personal affairs and property of an individual incapable of those duties; for example, an orphaned child.

Guest-to-car ratio The number of parking spaces allotted for each living unit for guest use; typically used in urban planning for high-density housing.

Habitable In a condition appropriate for human occupation.

Habitable room A room used for living purposes; bathrooms and hallways are not considered habitable rooms. Normally habitable rooms are the only rooms counted towards the number of rooms in a house.

Half section An area of land with 320 acres; considered one seventy-second of a township.

Handicap A physical or mental impairment that limits one or more life activities as defined by the fair housing act. Also referred to as a disability.

Hangout The remaining balance of a loan when the term of the loan is beyond the term of a lease. A property with a 20-year loan and a 15-year lease has a 5-year hangout.

Hard cost The expenses attributed to constructing property improvements.

Hard money mortgage A mortgage given to a borrower in exchange for cash rather than a mortgage secured by real estate. Pledging equity in a property against a loan is considered a hard money mortgage.

Hazard insurance Also known as homeowners insurance or fire insurance. A policy that provides coverage for damage from forces such as fire and wind.

Hearing A formal procedure with issues of fact or law to be tried and settled. Similar to a trial and can result in a final order.

Heavy industry Businesses that require sufficient property to accommodate their function. Factories, mills, or manufacturing facilities are considered heavy industry. Noise, pollution, and heavy truck traffic are often the result of heavy industry.

Hectare A metric land measurement equal to 2.471 acres, or 107,637 square feet.

Height The height of a building is the distance from the curb or grade level, whichever is higher, to the highest level of a flat root or to the average height of a pitched roof.

Heir One who might inherit or succeed to an interest in land under the state law of descent when the owner dies without leaving a valid will.

Heirs and assigns Heirs are recipients of an inheritance from a deceased owner; assigns are successors in interest to a property. Usually found in deeds and wills. To will property to heirs and assigns means the person receiving the property can then sell it or will it to his or her own heirs.

Hereditament Any property—real or personal, tangible or intangible—that may be inherited.

Hiatus A gap in the chain of title; a space existing between adjoining parcels of land due to a faulty legal description.

Hidden defect A title defect that is not apparent from examination of the public record. A secret marriage can be a cause of a hidden defect.

High rise In a suburban district, any building taller than six stories. In a business district, any building taller than 25 stories.

High water mark The line on the shore that marks the level of a medium tide; denotes the boundary of property between a parcel of land and a public waterway.

Highest and best use The most reasonable, expected, legal use of a piece of vacant land or improved property that is physically possible, supported appropriately, financially feasible, and that results in the highest value.

Highway A road that serves continuing traffic and is the primary route between communities

Historic structure A building that is officially recognized for historic significance and has special tax status.

Hold harmless clause A clause in a contract where one party agrees to protect the other party from claims. Protects the other party from lawsuits; for example, a landlord of a commercial property may include a hold harmless clause that indemnifies them from actions taken by customers of the tenant.

Hold over tenant A tenant who retains possession of the leased premises after the lease has expired.

Holdbacks A portion of a loan funding that is not dispersed until an additional condition is met, such as the completion of construction.

Holder in due course A person who acquires a bearer instrument in good faith and is eligible to keep it even though it may have been stolen. Also refers to a person who has obtained a negotiable instrument without knowledge that it may be defective.

Holding company A company that owns or controls another company or companies.

Holding escrow An arrangement where an escrow agent holds the final title documents to a title for deed.

Holding period The expected length of time, from purchase to sale, that an investor will own a property.

Holdover tenancy A tenancy whereby a lessee retains possession of leased property after the lease has expired and the landlord, by continuing to accept rent, agrees to the tenant's continued occupancy as defined by state law.

Holiday Legally recognized or widely recognized days when state and federal offices and banks and lending institutions typically are not open for business.

Holographic will A will that is written, dated, and signed in the testator's handwriting.

Home Equity Conversion Mortgage (HECM) Also referred to as a Reverse Annuity Mortgage. A type of mortgage in which the lender makes payments to the owner, thereby enabling older homeowners to convert equity in their homes into cash in the form of monthly payments.

Home equity line An open-ended amount of credit based on the equity a homeowner has accumulated.

Home equity loan A loan (sometimes called a line of credit) under which a property owner uses his or her residence as collateral and can then draw funds up to a prearranged amount against the property.

Home inspection A pre-purchase examination of the condition a home is in by a certified inspector.

Home Inspector A certified professional who determines the structural soundness and operating systems of a property.

Home ownership Living in a structure owned by the resident.

Home price The price that a buyer and seller agree upon, generally based on the home's appraised market value.

Homeowners Association (HOA) A group that governs a community, condominium building, or neighborhood and enforces the covenants, conditions, and restrictions set by the developer.

Homeowners association dues The monthly payments that are paid to the homeowners' association for maintenance and communal expenses.

Homeowners insurance A policy that includes coverage for all damages that may affect the value of a house as defined in the terms of the insurance policy.

Homeowners insurance policy A standardized package insurance policy that covers a residential real estate owner against financial loss from fire, theft, public liability, and other common risks.

Homeowners warranty A type of policy homebuyers often purchase to cover repairs, such as heating or air conditioning, should they stop working within the coverage period.

Homestead Land that is owned and occupied as the family home. In many states a portion of the area or value of this land is protected or exempt from judgments for debts.

Homogeneous Uniform; of like characteristics or quality.

Horizontal property laws State statutes that enable condominium ownership of property.

Hostile possession Possession of real property by one person that is adverse to the possession of the title owner. Hostile possession does not recognize the title of the true owner.

House poor An expression used to indicate that a major portion of a person's income goes to housing expenses, leaving little for other expenses.

House rules Rules of conduct adopted by the board of a condominium owners association; designed to create harmonious living among owners and occupants.

Housing Expense Ratio (HER) The percentage of gross income that is devoted to housing costs each month.

Housing for the elderly A project specifically designed for persons 55 and older providing accommodations and common use space.

Housing starts An estimate of the number of dwelling units on which construction has begun or will begin during a specific period.

HUD Housing and Urban Development. A federal agency that oversees a variety of housing and community development programs, including the FHA.

HUD median income The average income for families in a particular area, which is estimated by HUD.

HUD-1 Settlement Statement Also known as the Closing Statement or Settlement Sheet. An itemized listing of the funds paid at closing.

Hundred percent location A term that refers to a location in the downtown business district of a city or town that commands the highest land value. Typically reflects the highest rental prices and the highest traffic and pedestrian flow.

HVAC Heating, Ventilating, and Air Conditioning.

Hybrid debt A position in a mortgage that has equity-like features of participation in both cash flow and the appreciation of the property at the point of sale or refinance.

Hypothecate To pledge property as security for an obligation or loan without giving up possession of it.

Idem sonans Latin phrase for "sounding the same." Names spelled improperly, for example, do not necessarily void a contract.

Illiquidity Inadequate cash on hand to meet operations. Real estate is generally considered illiquid because it is difficult to convert it quickly to cash.

Impact fees An expense charged to private developers by the city as a condition for granting permission for a specific project. The purpose of the fee is to defray the cost of extending public services, like water or sewer lines, to the development.

Implied agency Based on the actions of the parties which imply that they have mutually consented to an agency relationship, an implied agency relationship is formed.

Implied agreement A contract under which the agreement of the parties is demonstrated by their acts and conduct.

Implied cap rate The net operating income divided by the sum of a REIT's equity market capitalization and its total outstanding debt.

Implied contract See implied agreement.

Implied listing An agreement under which the agreement of the parties is demonstrated by their acts and conduct.

Implied warranty of habitability A theory in landlord/tenant law in which the landlord renting residential property implies that the property is habitable and fit for its intended use.

Impound account Similar to an escrow account; established to set aside funds for future needs relating to a property.

Impounds The part of the monthly mortgage payment that is reserved in an account to pay for hazard insurance, property taxes, and private mortgage insurance.

Improved land Land that has some improvements, or land that has been partially or fully developed for use. A lot with a well installed is considered to be improved land, even though it is not yet suitable for habitation.

Improvement Any structure, usually privately owned, erected on a site to enhance the value of the property—for example, building a fence or a driveway; publicly owned structure added to or benefiting land, such as a curb, sidewalk, street, or sewer.

Improvements The upgrades or changes made to a building to improve its value or usefulness.

Imputed interest Interest implied by law. Interest is imputed when the stated terms specify an interest rate too low for market conditions.

Imputed notice An agent's knowledge that is binding on the principal because of an agency relationship between them. If a buyer's agent is notified of the acceptance of an offer, the buyer cannot withdraw the offer even if he or she did not have actual notice of the acceptance by the buyer's agent.

In house sale A sale in which the listing broker is the only broker in the transaction. The listing broker may have found the buyer or another salesperson working for the broker found by the buyer.

Incentive fee A rate structure in which the fee amount charged is based on the performance of the real estate assets under management.

Inchoate Unfinished; begun but not completed.

Income approach The process of estimating the value of an income-producing property through capitalization of the annual net income expected to be produced by the property during its remaining useful life.

Income capitalization value The figure derived for an income-producing property by converting its expected benefits into property value.

Income property A particular property that is used to generate income but is not occupied by the owner.

Income return The percentage of the total return generated by the income from property, fund, or account operations.

Income statement A historical financial report indicating the sources and amounts of revenues, amounts of expenses, and profits or losses. Can be prepared on an accrual or a cash basis.

Incompetent A person not legally capable of completing a contract. Includes minors, mentally ill, and others not considered capable by law.

Incorporate To form a corporation under state regulations.

Incorporation by reference A method of including the terms of other documents into another document simply by referencing those documents.

Incorporeal right A non-possessory right in real estate; for example, an easement or a right-of-way.

Increment An increase in quantity or size; commonly used to refer to the development of large subdivisions in phases.

Incubator space An industrial park or building subdivided into small units to house small, growing companies who wish to share office, clerical, or meeting room space.

Incurable obsolescence A defect that either cannot be cured or is not financially practical to cure. If curing a structural problem will cost more than the property is worth, the problem is considered an incurable obsolescence.

Indemnify To protect another person against loss or damage.

Indenture A written agreement made between two or more persons who have different interests; a deed in which both parties bind themselves to reciprocal obligations.

Independent contractor Someone who is retained to perform a certain act but who is subject to the control and direction of another only as to the end result and not as to the way in which the act is performed. Unlike an employee, an independent contractor pays for all expenses and Social Security and income taxes and receives no employee benefits. Most real estate salespeople are independent contractors.

Index A financial table that lenders use for calculating interest rates on ARMs.

Index loan A long term loan in which the payment terms may be adjusted based on changes in a specified index.

Index method The appraisal method of estimating building costs by multiplying the original cost of the property by a percentage factor to adjust for current construction costs.

Indexed rate The sum of the published index with a margin added.

Indicated value The worth of a subject property as shown in the three basic approaches to value: recent sales of comparable properties, cost less accrued depreciation plus land value, and capitalization of annual net operating income.

Indirect costs Expenses of development other than the costs of direct material and labor that are related directly to the construction of improvements.

Indirect lighting Light that is reflected from the ceiling or other object external to the fixture.

Individual account management The process of maintaining accounts that have been established for individual plan sponsors or other investors for investment in real estate, where a firm acts as an adviser in obtaining and/or managing a real estate portfolio.

Indoor air quality The presence (or lack of) pollutants in a building, such as tobacco smoke, carbon monoxide, radon, and asbestos.

Industrial broker A real estate broker specializing in brokering industrial real estate.

Industrial park An area designed and zoned for manufacturing and associated businesses and activities.

Inflation The gradual reduction of the purchasing power of the dollar, usually related directly to the increases in the money supply by the federal government; the rate at which consumer prices increase each year.

Inflation hedge An investment whose value tends to increase at a greater rate than inflation, contributing to the preservation of the purchasing power of a portfolio.

Informed consent Consent to a certain act that is given after a full and fair disclosure of all facts needed to make a conscious choice.

Infrastructure The basic public works of a city or subdivision, including roads, bridges, sewer systems, water systems, and public utilities.

Ingress The right to enter; egress is the right to exit.

Inheritance taxes State-imposed taxes on a decedent's real and personal property.

Initial interest rate The original interest rate on an ARM which is sometimes subject to a variety of adjustments throughout the mortgage.

Initial Public Offering (IPO) The first time a previously private company offers securities for public sale.

Initial rate cap The limit specified by some ARMs as the maximum amount the interest rate may increase when the initial interest rate expires.

Initial rate duration The date specified by most ARMs at which the initial rate expires.

Initials Abbreviation for a name. Initials are often used as a person's signature.

Injunction A legal action where a court issues a writ that forbids a party from committing an act or compels a party to perform an act.

Inner city An urban area that is generally recognized as a central residential or commercial part of a city.

Innocent misrepresentation A misstatement of fact made without the intent to deceive.

Innocent purchaser A party who is not responsible for cleanup of contaminated property. Applies to a party who knew nothing about the contamination and had an investigation performed before the purchase.

Inquiry notice Notice the law presumes a reasonable person would obtain by inquiring into a property.

Inside lot A lot surrounded on each side by other lots, with road frontage on one side; a corner lot has road frontage on two sides.

Inspection Physical scrutiny of a property or of documents.

Inspection fee The fee that a licensed property inspector charges for determining the current physical condition of the property.

Inspection report A written report of the property's condition presented by a licensed inspection professional.

Installment contract A contract for the sale of real estate whereby the purchase price is paid in periodic installments by the purchaser, who is in possession of the property even though title is retained by the seller until a future date, which may be not until final payment. Also called a "contract for deed" or "articles of agreement for warranty deed."

Installment note A promissory note providing for payment of principal in two or more stated amounts, at different times.

Installment sale A transaction in which the sales price is paid in two or more installments over two or more years. If the sale meets certain requirements, a taxpayer can postpone reporting such income until future years by paying tax each year only on the proceeds received that year.

Institutional grade property A variety of types of real estate properties usually owned or financed by tax-exempt institutional investors.

Institutional lender Financial intermediaries who invest in loans and other securities on behalf of investors or depositors; loans made by institutional lenders are regulated by law.

Instrument A written legal document created to establish the rights and liabilities of the parties to it.

Insulation Materials used to slow the transfer of heat or cold through walls, reducing energy costs, and maintaining a consistent temperature.

Insulation disclosure The requirement that real estate brokers, builders, and sellers of new houses must disclose the type, thickness, and R-value of insulation in the house.

Insurable interest An interest in a person or property that would cause one a loss if that person or property were injured. A lender can collect on an insurance policy because the lender has an interest in the property.

Insurable title A title that can be insured by a title insurance company.

Insurance Indemnification against loss from specific perils. Fire insurance, for example, indemnifies the purchaser against losses due to fire.

Insurance binder A temporary insurance policy that is implemented while a permanent policy is drawn up or obtained.

Insurance company separate account A real estate investment vehicle only offered by life insurance companies, which enables an ERISA-governed fund to avoid creating unrelated taxable income for certain types of property investments and investment structures.

Insured mortgage A mortgage that is guaranteed by the FHA or by private mortgage insurance (PMI).

Inter vivos During one's life.

Inter vivos trust A trust set up during one's lifetime.

Interest A charge made by a lender for the use of money; the cost for the use of money.

Interest accrual rate The rate at which a mortgage accrues interest.

Interest in property A legal share of ownership in a property.

Interest only loan A mortgage for which the borrower pays only the interest that accrues on the loan balance each month.

Interest only strip A derivative security that consists of all or part of the portion of interest in the underlying loan or security.

Interest paid over life of loan The total amount that has been paid to the lender during the time the money was borrowed.

Interest rate The percentage that is charged for a loan.

Interest rate buy down plans A plan in which a seller uses funds from the sale of the home to buy down the interest rate and reduce the buyer's monthly payments.

Interest rate cap The highest interest rate charge allowed on the monthly payment of an ARM during an adjustment period.

Interest rate ceiling The maximum interest rate a lender can charge for an ARM.

Interest rate floor The minimum possible interest rate a lender can charge for an ARM.

Interim financing Also known as Bridge or Swing Loans. Short-term financing a seller uses to bridge the gap between the sale of one house and the purchase of another.

Interlocutory decree A judicial order that does not take final effect until a specified time or until a specified event occurs.

Intermediate theory The concept that a mortgage is a lien on property until default, at which time title passes to the lender.

Internal Rate of Return (IRR) The calculation of a discounted cash-flow analysis which is used to determine the potential total return of a real estate asset during a particular holding period.

Internal revenue code The law passed by Congress that specifies how and what income is to be taxed and what may be deducted from taxable income.

Interpleader A proceeding initiated by a neutral third party to determine the rights of rival claimants to a property or a transaction.

Interstate Occurring between two or more states, triggering the jurisdiction of federal law.

Interstate Land Sales Full Disclosure Act A federal law that regulates the sale of certain real estate in interstate commerce.

Interval ownership Time share ownership where the owner acquires title to a specific unit for a certain week or weeks per year.

Intestate The condition of a property owner who dies without leaving a valid will. Title to the property will pass to the decedent's heirs as provided in the state law of descent.

Intrastate exemption Having made no valid will; a person who dies leaving no will, or leaving a defective will.

Intrinsic value An appraisal term referring to the value created by a person's personal preferences for a particular type of property.

Inventory The entire space of a certain proscribed market without concern for its availability or condition.

Inverse condemnation An action brought by a property owner seeking just compensation for land taken for public use when the taker of the property does not intend to bring eminent domain proceedings. Property is condemned because its use and value have been diminished due to an adjacent property's public use.

Investment Money directed toward the purchase, improvement, and development of an asset in expectation of income or profits.

Investment committee The governing body that is charged with overseeing corporate pension investments and developing investment policies for board approval.

Investment manager An individual or company that assumes authority over a specified amount of real estate capital, invests that capital in assets using a separate account, and provides asset management.

Investment policy A document that formalizes an institution's goals, objectives, and guidelines for asset management, investment advisory contracting, fees, and utilization of consultants and other outside professionals.

Investment property A piece of real estate that generates some form of income.

Investment strategy The methods used by a manager in structuring a portfolio and selecting the real estate assets for a fund or an account.

Investment structures Approaches to investing that include unleveraged acquisitions, leveraged acquisitions, traditional debt, participating debt, convertible debt, triple-net leases, and joint ventures.

Investment-Grade CMBS Commercial Mortgage-Backed Securities that have ratings of AAA, AA, A, or BBB.

Investor status The position an investor is in, either taxable and tax-exempt.

Involuntary conversion Condemnation or sudden destruction by nature. A property can be involuntarily converted through eminent domain, or be destroyed by a natural disaster.

Involuntary lien A lien placed on property without the consent of the property owner; a mechanics lien is an example of an involuntary lien.

Inwood tables A set of tables used by appraisers used to compute the present value of an annuity for a number of years at various interest rates.

Ironclad agreement An agreement that cannot be broken by any of the parties involved.

Irrevocable consent An agreement that cannot be withdrawn or revoked.

Joint and several liability A phrase meaning that each of the individual owners is personally responsible for the total damages.

Joint liability The condition in which responsibility rests with two or more people for fulfilling the terms of a home loan or other financial debt.

Joint tenancy A form of ownership in which two or more people have equal shares in a piece of property, and rights pass to the surviving owner(s) in the event of death.

Joint venture The joining of two or more people to conduct a specific business enterprise. A joint venture is similar to a partnership in that it must be created by agreement between the parties to share in the losses and profits of the venture. It is unlike a partnership in that the venture is for one specific project only, rather than for a continuing business relationship.

Judgment The formal decision of a court upon the respective rights and claims of the parties to an action or suit. After a judgment has been entered and recorded with the county recorder, it usually becomes a general lien on the property of the defendant.

Judgment lien The claim on a property of a debtor resulting from a judgment.

Judgment proof Having no assets that will satisfy a judgment for money.

Judicial foreclosure The usual foreclosure proceeding some states use, which is handled in a civil lawsuit.

Judicial precedent In law, the requirements established by prior court decisions.

Jumbo loan A type of mortgage that exceeds the required limits set by Fannie Mae and Freddie Mac. Jumbo loans must be maintained in the lender's portfolio or be sold to private investors.

Junior lien An obligation, such as a second mortgage, that is subordinate in right or lien priority to an existing lien on the same realty.

Junior mortgage A loan that is a lower priority, behind and after the primary loan.

Jurat The clause at the bottom of an affidavit made by a notary public stating when, where, and before whom an affidavit was sworn.

Jurisdiction Area of authority for a specific government agency or entity.

Just compensation The amount that is fair to both the owner and the government when property is appropriated for public use through Eminent Domain.

Key employee insurance A life insurance policy, paid for by the company, to cover the cost of replacing a key person in the company. A key employee policy can either be a life insurance policy, a disability policy, or both.

Key lot A lot that has added value because of its strategic location, especially when it is needed for the highest and best use of contiguous property. A key lot is also a lot that adjoins the rear property line of a corner lot and fronts on a secondary street.

Key money A payment made to secure a leasing interest. The tenant is in effect purchasing the "key" to the property.

Key tenant A major office building tenant that leases several floors, or a major department store in a shopping center.

Kickers Payment required by a mortgage in addition to normal principal and interest.

Kitchenette A space less than 60 square feet that is used for cooking and preparing food.

Knockdown Pre-manufactured construction materials delivered to the building site unassembled; can be quickly assembled and installed.

Laches Undue delay or negligence in asserting legal rights, possibly leading to estoppel of a negligent party's suit.

Lanai Popular term used in western and southern states referring to a balcony, veranda, porch, or covered patio.

Land The earth's surface, extending downward to the center of the earth and upward infinitely into space, including things permanently attached by nature, such as trees and water.

Land bank Land purchased and held for future development.

Land banker Developer who improves raw land for construction purposes and who maintains an inventory of improved lots for future purposes.

Land capacity The ability of land to handle labor and capital improvements.

Land contract An installment contract for sale with the buyer receiving equitable title (a right to possession) and the seller retaining legal title. Similar to a contract for deed.

Land description Legal description of a particular piece of real estate.

Land economics Economic study concentrating on the economic attributes of land and the economics of agriculture.

Land grant Grant of public lands by the government, usually for roads, railroads, or agricultural colleges.

Land leaseback Only the ground is covered by the lease. Structures built on the land revert to the original owner at the termination of the lease.

Land poor Short of money because the expense of owning property does not produce enough income to cover operating costs.

Land residual technique An appraisal method where the value of land is estimated by comparing the net operating income and the value of improvements. Typically used for feasibility analyses and to determine the highest and best use of a piece of land.

Land trust A trust originated by the owner of real property in which real estate is the only asset.

Land use intensity A measure of the extent to which a land parcel is developed.

Land use map A map that shows the types and intensities of different land uses in a particular area.

Land, tenements and hereditaments A federal phrase used to describe all types of "immovable" real estate, including land, buildings, and rights; the complete ownership of the bundle of rights in a property.

Landlocked A lot that has no access to a public road or highway except through an adjacent lot.

Landlord A person or company who rents property to another person; a landlord is the lessor.

Landlords warrant The warrant a landlord obtains to take a tenant's personal property to sell at a public sale to compel payment of the rent or other stipulation in the lease.

Landmark A fixed object serving as a boundary mark for a tract of land. A landmark is also considered to be a monument.

Landscaping Shrubs, bushes, trees, and other plants surrounding a structure.

Lane A narrow road without curbs or sidewalks.

Larger parcel Property from which condemned property is taken. The larger parcel includes property that is affected by the taking through eminent domain, but not actually taken, and severance damages are calculated.

Late charge The fee that is imposed by a lender when the borrower has not made a payment when it was due.

Late payment The payment made to the lender after the due date has passed.

Latent defect A hidden structural defect that could not be discovered by ordinary inspection and that threatens the property's soundness or the safety of its inhabitants. Some states impose on sellers and licensees a duty to inspect for and disclose latent defects.

Lateral and subjacent support The support a parcel of real estate receives from land adjoining it.

Law day The date an obligation becomes due.

Lawful interest The maximum interest rate permitted by law, with any amount above the statutory rate considered to be usurious.

Leaching cesspool A cesspool that is not watertight and permits liquids to pass into the surrounding soil.

Lead lender A lender who finances the initial portion of a large loan and arranges for other institutional or private investors to fund the balance of the financing. Typically the lead lender handles the servicing of the loan.

Lead manager The investment banking firm that has primary responsibility for coordinating the new issuance of securities.

Lead poisoning Serious illness caused by high concentrations of lead in the body.

Leaking underground storage tank (LUST) An underground storage tank that is not watertight and permits liquids to pass into the surrounding soil.

Lease A written or oral contract between a landlord (the lessor) and a tenant (the lessee) that transfers the right to exclusive possession and use of the landlord's real property to the lessee for a specified period of time and for a stated consideration (rent). By state law leases for longer than a certain period of time (generally one year) must be in writing to be enforceable.

Lease commencement date The date at which the terms of the lease are implemented.

Lease expiration exposure schedule A chart of the total square footage of all current leases that expire in each of the next five years, without taking renewal options into account.

Lease option A financing option that provides for homebuyers to lease a home with an option to buy, with part of the rental payments being applied toward the down payment.

Lease purchase The purchase of real property, the consummation of which is preceded by a lease, usually long-term. Typically used for tax or financing purposes.

Lease purchase A lease that gives the tenant the right to purchase the property at an agreed-upon price under certain conditions.

Leasehold estate A tenant's right to occupy real estate during the term of a lease, generally considered to be a personal property interest.

Leasehold improvements Fixtures attached to real estate that are purchased or installed by the tenant. When the lease expires, the tenant is generally allowed to remove those improvements, provided the removal does not damage the property.

Leasehold interest The right to hold or use property for a specific period of time at a given price without transferring ownership.

Leasehold mortgage A lien on the tenant's interest in real estate.

Leasehold state A way of holding a property title in which the mortgagor does not actually own the property but has a long-term lease on it.

Leeward On or towards the side sheltered from the wind; opposite of windward.

Legacy A disposition of money or personal property by will.

Legal age The standard of maturity upon which a party is held legally responsible for that party's acts. The legal age for real estate transactions is 18.

Legal blemish A negative count against a piece of property such as a zoning violation or fraudulent title claim.

Legal description A description of a specific parcel of real estate complete enough for an independent surveyor to locate and identify it.

Legal name The name an individual has for legal purposes.

Legal notice Notification of others using the method required by law. For example, a deed recorded in the local courthouse is a legal notice of ownership.

Legal owner The party who holds the title to the property, although the title may carry no actual rights to the property other than as a lien.

Legal rate of interest The rate of interest prescribed by state law that prevails in the absence of an agreement stating the rate of interest.

Legally competent parties People who are recognized by law as being able to contract with others; those of legal age and sound mind.

Legatee A person who receives property by will.

Lender Any party who originates or holds loans.

Less than freehold estate An estate in land that has a predetermined time span; most commonly called a leasehold.

Lessee A person to whom property is rented under a lease.

Lessor A person who rents property to another under a lease.

Let To rent property to a tenant.

Letter of credit A promise from a bank or other party that the issuer will honor drafts or other requests for payment upon complying with the requirements specified in the letter of credit.

Letter of intent An initial agreement defining the proposed terms for the end contract.

Letter of patent A legal instrument transferring title to real property from either the government or an individual state to an individual.

Letter report A short appraisal report limited to property characteristics, valuation, and recommendation; a report by a title company as to the condition of the title on a specific date. A letter report gives no insurance on that title.

Level payment mortgage A mortgage requiring the same payment each month until full amortization. Also called a flat mortgage.

Leverage The use of borrowed money to finance an investment.

Levy To assess; to seize or collect. To levy a tax is to assess a property and set the rate of taxation. To levy an execution is to seize the property of a person to satisfy an obligation.

Liabilities A borrower's debts and financial obligations, whether long- or short-term.

Liability insurance A type of policy that protects owners against negligence, personal injury, or property damage claims.

LIBOR Acronym for London Interbank Offered Rate. An index used to determine interest rate changes for adjustable rate mortgages. Very popular index for interest only mortgage programs.

License A privilege or right granted to a person by a state to operate as a real estate broker or salesperson; the revocable permission for a temporary use of land, a personal right that cannot be sold.

Lien A claim put on property, making it security for payment of a debt, judgment, mortgage, or taxes.

Lien statement A statement of the unpaid balance of a promissory note secured by a lien on property, plus the status of interest payments, maturity date, and any claims that may be asserted. A lien statement is also called an offset statement.

Lien theory Some states interpret a mortgage as being purely a lien on real property. The mortgagee thus has no right of possession but must foreclose the lien and sell the property if the mortgagor defaults.

Lien theory states States whose laws give a lien on property to secure date. In a title theory state, the lender becomes the title owner. In either case the lenders may foreclose in the event of default.

Lien waiver A waiver of a mechanic's lien rights that is sometimes required before the general contractor can receive money under the payment provisions of a construction loan and contract.

Life cap A limit on the amount an ARM's interest rate can increase during the mortgage term.

Life care facility A residential development designed to provide medical and nursing care for senior citizens.

Life cycle costing In property management, comparing one type of equipment with another based on both purchase cost and operating cost over its expected useful lifetime.

Life estate An interest in real or personal property that is limited in duration to the lifetime of its owner or some other designated person or persons.

Life tenant A person in possession of a life estate limited partnership. See partnership.

Lifecycle The stages of development for a property: pre-development, development, leasing, operating, and rehabilitation.

Lifetime payment cap A limit on the amount that payments can increase or decrease over the life of an ARM.

Lifetime rate cap The highest possible interest rate that may be charged, under any circumstances, over the entire life of an ARM.

Light and air The principle stating that an owner has no natural right to light and air and cannot complain when a neighbor erects a structure that cuts off his or her light and air.

Light industry Zoning designation referring to industrial use encompassing mostly light manufacturing businesses that do not cause noise, air, or water disturbances or pollution.

Like kind property Property having the same nature.

Limitations of actions Time within which legal actions must commence or else those actions will be barred or disallowed. Similar to a statute of limitations.

Limited access highway A highway with access only at specific intervals, usually through the use of on and off ramps. Also called a controlled access highway.

Limited liability company A form of ownership treated as a partnership for federal tax purposes with limited liability protection for owners.

Limited partnership A type of partnership in which some partners manage the business and are personally liable for partnership debts, but some partners contribute capital and share in profits without the responsibility of management.

Limited power of attorney A power of attorney that is limited to a specific task or set of tasks; does not confer general authority to act on the behalf of another party.

Limited referral agent A salesperson with an active real estate license who refers prospective buyers or sellers to a brokerage company in return for a referral fee at closing.

Limited warranty deed A deed containing warranties covering the time period the grantor holds title.

Line of credit An amount of credit granted by a financial institution up to a specified amount for a certain period of time to a borrower.

Line of sight easement A right that restricts the use of land within the easement area in any way that will restrict the view.

Line stakes Stakes set along boundary lines of a parcel of land.

Lineal foot A measure of one foot, in a straight line, along the ground.

Liquid asset A type of asset that can be easily converted into cash.

Liquidated damages An amount predetermined by the parties to a contract as the total compensation to an injured party should the other party breach the contract.

Liquidity The ease with which an individual's or company's assets can be converted to cash without losing their value.

Lis pendens Latin for "pending suit." A recorded notice of the filing of a suit.

Listing agreement An agreement between a property owner and a real estate broker which authorizes the broker to attempt to sell or lease the property at a specified price and terms in return for a commission or other compensation.

Listing broker The listing broker is the broker in a multiple-listing situation from whose office a listing agreement is initiated. The listing broker and the cooperating broker may be the same person.

Litigation The act of engaging in or carrying on a lawsuit.

Littoral Part of the shore zone of a large body of water. Land bordering on the shore of a sea or ocean and thus affected by tide currents.

Littoral rights A landowner's claim to use water in large navigable lakes and oceans adjacent to his or her property; the ownership rights to land bordering these bodies of water up to the high-water mark.

Livability space ratio The minimum square footage of outdoor area in a development that is provided for each square foot of total floor area.

Living trust An arrangement in which a property owner, called the trustor, transfers assets to a trustee who assumes specified duties in managing the asset.

Loan An amount of money that is borrowed and usually repaid with interest; an offer of borrowed money; an agreement for debt financing.

Loan application A document that presents a borrower's income, debt, and other obligations to determine creditworthiness, as well as some basic information on the target property.

Loan application fee A fee lenders charge to cover expenses relating to reviewing a loan application.

Loan balance table A table showing the balance remaining to be paid on an amortized loan. Sometimes called a remaining balance table.

Loan commitment An agreement by a lender or other financial institution to make or insure a loan for the specified amount and terms.

Loan correspondent Person who negotiates loans for conventional lending institutions or other lenders. Correspondents often service the loan for the lender and act as the collecting agents.

Loan officer An official representative of a lending institution who is authorized to act on behalf of the lender within specified limits.

Loan origination The process of obtaining and arranging new loans.

Loan origination fee A fee charged to the borrower by the lender for making a mortgage loan. The fee is usually computed as a percentage of the loan amount.

Loan package The collection of documents associated with a specific loan application.

Loan servicing The process a lending institution goes through for all loans it manages. This involves processing payments, sending statements, managing the escrow/impound account, providing collection services on delinquent loans, ensuring that insurance and property taxes are made on the property, handling pay-offs and assumptions, as well as various other services.

Loan submission The package of papers and documents supporting a loan application received by a lender for review and consideration.

Loan term The time, usually expressed in years, that a lender sets in which a buyer must pay a mortgage.

Loan To Value ratio (LTV) The relationship between the amount of the mortgage loan and the value of the real estate being pledged as collateral.

Lobby Public waiting area or meeting place used as a common area by tenants or guests.

Location, location, location A popular statement that emphasizes the location of a property in determining its value. Often phrased as, "The three most important considerations in real estate are location, location, location."

Lock box structure An arrangement in which the payments are sent directly from the tenant or borrower to the trustee.

Lock boxes A special lock placed at a property for sale containing a key to the property; can only be opened by agents with a key to the lock box.

Lock in A commitment from a lender to a borrower to guarantee a given interest rate for a limited amount of time.

Lock-in clause A condition in a promissory that prohibits early payoff of a note.

Lock-in period The period of time during which the borrower is guaranteed a specified interest rate.

Lockout period The period of time during which a loan may not be paid off early.

Loft A building area that is unfinished; open space on the first or second floor typically used for manufacturing or retail operations.

London InterBank Offered Rate (LIBOR) The interest rate offered on Eurodollar deposits traded between banks and used to determine changes in interest rate for ARMs.

Long-term lease A rental agreement that will last at least three years from initial signing to the date of expiration or renewal.

Loop A looped roadway having two access points off the same roadway.

Loss payee The person designated on an insurance policy as the one to be paid in case the property is damaged or destroyed. A secured lender often requires a borrower to carry adequate insurance on property used as security, and requires the borrower to name the lender as the loss payee.

Loss severity The percentage of lost principal when a loan is foreclosed.

Lot An individual parcel of land in a subdivision; one of several contiguous parcels of a larger piece of land.

Lot and block (recorded plat) system A method of describing real property that identifies a parcel of land by reference to lot and block numbers within a subdivision, as specified on a recorded subdivision plat.

Lot split Division of land by separating its ownership or dividing it into several parcels.

Low documentation loan A mortgage that requires only a basic verification of income and assets.

Low rise A building that involves fewer than four stories above the ground level.

Luminous ceiling A ceiling emitting light from its entire surface through the use of fluorescent light above translucent glass or plastic.

Lump-sum contract A type of construction contract that requires the general contractor to complete a building project for a fixed cost that is usually established beforehand by competitive bidding.

Lump-sum payment Repayment of a debt by a single payment, including principal and any accrued interest. A note may provide for periodic interest payments and one lump-sum principal payment, for example.

Maggie Mae (MGIC) Nickname for Mortgage Guaranty Insurance Corporation (MGIC), which insures mortgages to other investors.

Magic page A story of projected growth which describes how a new REIT will achieve its future plans for funds from operations or funds available for distribution.

Magic wrap A mortgaging procedure in which MGIC insures a mortgage and sells it on the secondary market when the mortgage wraps around an existing VA or FHA mortgage.

MAI A professional designation that signifies the appraiser is qualified to appraise a broad range of real estate types.

Maintenance Activities required to compensate for or overcome wear and tear on a property.

Maintenance fee The charge to homeowners' association members each month for the repair and maintenance of common areas.

Majority The age at which a person is no longer a minor; majority is 18 to 21 years of age depending on the state. A majority can also be more than half.

Maker One who issues a promissory note and commits to paying the note when it is due.

Malfeasance Commission of an act that is clearly unlawful.

Mall A public area connecting individual stores in a shopping center. A mall is generally enclosed.

Management agreement A contract between the owner of income property and a management firm or individual property manager that outlines the scope of the manager's authority.

Maps and plats Surveys of pieces of land showing monuments, boundaries, area, ownership, and other features.

Margin A constant amount that is added to the value of an index for the purpose of adjusting the interest rate on an adjustable rate mortgage; a percentage that is added to the index and fixed for the mortgage term.

Marginal land Land that is barely profitable to use.

Marginal tax rate The ordinary rate of income tax charged on the last dollar of income; generally used to estimate calculations for investment decisions.

Marina A docking and mooring facility for boats, usually equipped with repair facilities, gas, and supplies.

Marital deduction The tax-free amount a person transfers by will to his or her spouse. Current tax laws allow an unlimited amount to be transferred without federal estate tax.

Mark to market The act of changing the original investment cost or value of a property or portfolio to the level of the current estimated market value.

Market A place where goods can be bought and sold and a price established.

Market capitalization A measurement of a company's value that is calculated by multiplying the current share price by the current number of shares outstanding.

Market conditions Features of the marketplace including interest rates, employment levels, demographics, vacancy rates, and absorption rates.

Market data approach An estimate of value obtained by comparing property being appraised with recently sold comparable properties.

Market rental rates The rental income that a landlord could most likely ask for a property in the open market, indicated by the current rents for comparable spaces.

Market study A forecast of the demand for a certain type of real estate project in the future which includes an estimate of the square footage that could be absorbed and the rents that could be charged.

Market value The price a property would sell for at a particular time in a competitive market.

Marketable title Good or clear title, reasonably free from the risk of litigation over possible defects.

Master deed A deed used by a condominium developer for recording a condominium development. Divides a single property into individually owned units.

Master lease The primary lease that controls other subsequent leases and may cover more property than all subsequent leases combined.

Master plan A comprehensive plan made by a government or government agency to guide the long-term physical development of a particular area.

Master Senior Appraiser (MSA) The senior designation granted by the National Association of Master Appraisers.

Master servicer An entity that acts on behalf of a trustee for security holders' benefit in collecting funds from a borrower, advancing funds in the event of delinquencies and, in the event of default, taking a property through foreclosure.

Master switch An electrical wall switch that controls more than one fixture or outlet in a room.

Materialman Supplier of materials used in the construction of an improvement.

Maturity The due date of a loan; the end of the period covered by a contract.

Maturity date The date at which the total principal balance of a loan is due.

Measure of damages The rule of law specifying the maximum amount of damages a plaintiff can recover for a breach of contract or other civil wrong.

Mechanics lien A claim created for securing payment priority for the price and value of work performed and materials furnished in constructing, repairing, or improving a building or other structure.

Meditation A process of dispute resolution where two parties work with an independent third party to attempt to resolve a difference.

Meeting of the minds Mutual assent or agreement between the parties to a contract.

Meeting space The space in hotels that is made available to the public to rent for meetings, conferences, or banquets.

Megan's Law Federal legislation that promotes the establishment of state registration systems to maintain residential information on every person who kidnaps children, commits sexual crimes against children, or commits sexually violent crimes.

Merged credit report A report that combines information from the three primary credit-reporting agencies including Equifax, Experian, and TransUnion.

Merger The fusion of two or more interests, such as businesses or investments.

Meridian One of a set of imaginary lines running north and south and crossing a base line at a definite point, used in the rectangular (government) survey system of property description.

Message The house and adjacent buildings and land used by a household.

Metes and bounds The surveyed boundary lines of a piece of land described by listing the compass directions (bounds) and distances (metes) of the boundaries.

Mezzanine An intermediate floor between two main stories of a building, or between the floor and ceiling of a one-story structure.

Mezzanine financing A financing position somewhere between equity and debt, meaning that there are higher-priority debts above and equity below.

Mid-rise A building which shows four to eight stories above ground level. In a business district, buildings up to 25 stories may also be considered mid rise buildings.

Middleman A person who brings two or more parties together, but does not conduct negotiations.

Mile 1,760 yards or 5,280 feet.

Military clause A provision in some leases allowing a tenant in military service to terminate the lease in the event of a transfer, discharge, or deployment.

Mill One-tenth of one cent. Some states use a mill rate to compute real estate taxes; for example, a rate of 52 mills would be $0.052 tax for each dollar of assessed valuation of a property.

Mineral rights The privilege of gaining income from the sale of oil, gas, and other valuable resources found on land.

Minimum lot area The smallest building lot area allowed in a subdivision.

Minimum property requirements Under FHA loan requirements, a property must be livable, soundly built, and suitably located as to site and location before the agency will underwrite a residential mortgage loan.

Minimum rent The smallest amount of rent from a tenant under a lease with a varying lease schedule.

Minor A person who has not reached the age of majority and therefore does not have legal capacity to transfer title to real property.

Misnomer A mistake in name.

Misplaced improvement A poorly located improvement, or an improvement that is poorly planned and detracts from the best use of the site.

Misrepresentation An untrue statement, whether intentional or unintentional.

Mistake An unintentional error made in preparing a contract; may be corrected by the consent of all parties without voiding the contract.

Mitigation of damages The obligation of the injured party to take reasonable steps to reduce or eliminate the amount of damages that party may be entitled to. A tenant is obligated to attempt to stop the flow of water from a broken pipe, for example to mitigate the damage.

Mixed use A term referring to space within a building or project which can be used for more than one activity.

Mobile home A dwelling unit manufactured in a factory and designed to be transported to a site and semi-permanently attached.

Model home A representative home used as part of a sales campaign to show the design, structure, and appearance of units in a development.

Modern Portfolio Theory (MPT) An approach of quantifying risk and return in an asset portfolio which emphasizes the portfolio rather than the individual assets and how the assets perform in relation to each other.

Modification An adjustment in the terms of a loan agreement.

Modified Annual Percentage Rate (APR) An index of the cost of a loan based on the standard APR but adjusted for the amount of time the borrower expects to hold the loan.

Modular housing Prefabricated housing manufactured at a location other than the actual lot, and transferred in sections to the lot for final construction.

Monetary policy Governmental regulation of the amount of money in circulation through such institutions as the Federal Reserve Board.

Month-to-month tenancy A periodic tenancy under which the tenant rents for one month at a time. In the absence of a rental agreement (oral or written) a tenancy is generally considered to be month to month. Some leases with fixed terms automatically convert to a month to month tenancy once the original term has expired.

Monthly association dues A payment due each month to a homeowners' association for expenses relating to maintenance and community operations.

Monument A fixed natural or artificial object used to establish real estate boundaries for a metes-and-bounds description.

Moral character The ability on the part of the person licensed to serve the public in a fair, honest, and ethical manner.

Moral turpitude An act of baseness, vileness, or depravity in private social duties; conduct contrary to justice, honesty, or good morals.

Moratorium A temporary suspension of payments; a time period during which certain activity is not allowed.

More or less When used in the description of real estate, a phrase indicating that the dimension or size given is approximate. Slight variation from the stated size will have no impact on the enforceability of the contract.

Mortgage An amount of money that is borrowed to purchase a property, using that property as collateral.

Mortgage acceleration clause A provision enabling a lender to require that the rest of the loan balance is paid in a lump sum under certain circumstances.

Mortgage backed security A bond or other financial obligation that is secured by a pool of mortgage loans.

Mortgage banker A financial institution that provides home loans using its own resources, often selling them to investors such as insurance companies or Fannie Mae.

Mortgage broker An individual who matches prospective borrowers with lenders that the broker is approved to deal with.

Mortgage broker business A company that matches prospective borrowers with lenders that the broker is approved to deal with.

Mortgage constant A figure comparing an amortizing mortgage payment to the outstanding mortgage balance.

Mortgage Insurance (MI) A policy, required by lenders on some loans, that covers the lender against certain losses that are incurred as a result of a default on a home loan.

Mortgage Insurance Premium (MIP) The amount charged for mortgage insurance, either to a government agency or to a private MI company.

Mortgage interest deduction The tax write-off that the IRS allows most homeowners to deduct for annual interest payments made on real estate loans.

Mortgage lien A lien or charge on the property of a mortgagor that secures the underlying debt obligations.

Mortgage life and disability insurance A type of term life insurance borrowers often purchase to cover debt that is left when the borrower dies or becomes too disabled to make the mortgage payments.

Mortgage pre-approval A process where a lender specifies that a borrower is financially qualified and creditworthy for a specific type of loan under specific terms and conditions.

Mortgage spreading agreement A contract that extends a previous mortgage lien to properties not previously covered, giving added security to the lender. Frequently used when the borrower seeks additional financing.

Mortgage subsidies Financing where a homebuilder permits the purchaser of a new home to occupy the home for a period of time without making monthly payments. The money saved goes toward down payments, and acts as a reserve to help make monthly payments once the financing is in place.

Mortgagee The lender (individual or company lending the money) in a mortgage loan transaction.

Mortgaging out Obtaining 100 percent of the money needed to acquire or develop a project. A person with 100 percent financing (no money down) has "mortgaged out."

Mortgagor The borrower (person receiving the money) in a mortgage loan transaction.

Mortmain The transfer of real property to a church, school, or charitable organization for perpetual ownership.

Most favored tenant clause A provision in a lease that assures a tenant that any negotiated concessions given to other subsequent clients will be extended to that tenant as well. Most favored tenant clauses help landlords in the early stages of renting, because it assures clients that later tenants will not receive better terms.

Mudroom A small room used as the entrance from a yard or play area. Many mudrooms contain a washer and dryer.

Mudsill The lowest horizontal component of a structure.

Multi-dwelling units A set of properties that provide separate housing areas for more than one family but only require a single mortgage.

Multi-peril policies Insurance policies that offer protection from a range of potential perils, such as those of a fire, hazard, public liability, and casualty.

Multiple dwelling A tenement house; any structure used for the accommodation of two or more households in separate living units; an apartment house.

Multiple listing An arrangement among a group of real estate brokers who agree in advance to provide information about some or all of their listings to the others, and who agree that commissions on sales of those listings will be split between listing and selling brokers.

Multiple listing clause A provision in an exclusive listing for the authority and obligation on the part of the listing broker to distribute the listing to other brokers in the multiple-listing organization.

Multiple Listing Service (MLS) A marketing organization composed of member brokers who agree to share their listing agreements with one another in the hope of procuring ready, willing, and able buyers for their properties more quickly than they could on their own. Most multiple-listing services accept exclusive-right-to-sell or exclusive-agency listings from their member brokers.

Multiple regression A technique used to estimate the value of a subject property based on known prices for comparable properties. Frequently used to create mass appraisals for single family residences.

Municipal ordinance Rules, regulations, and codes enacted into law by local governing bodies; typically cover building standards and subdivision requirements.

Mutual agreement The consent of all parties; consent of all parties to the provisions of a contract. Voluntary cancellation of a contract is referred to as mutual rescission.

Mutual savings bank Savings institutions that issue no stock and are mutually owned by their investors who are paid dividends on earnings and profit.

Mutual water company A water company organized for and operated by water users in a given district.

Mutuality of consent A meeting of the minds; a mutual assent of all parties to the formulation of the contract.

Naked title Title to a property lacking the usual rights and privileges of ownership.

Name, change of Use of a new name. Name changes performed subject to requirements are legal as long as no attempt is made to defraud or deceive others.

Name, reservation of The exclusive right to use a trade name or corporate name. The right is reserved by registering a corporation with state authorities.

Narrative report An appraisal report presented in descriptive paragraphs, as opposed to an appraisal presented in form, letter, or table format.

National Association of Exclusive Buyer Brokers A professional association of buyer brokers who specialize in the exclusive representation of buyers. They do not accept listings for sale.

National Association of Master Appraisers A professional association of appraisers formed to improve the practice of real estate appraising through mandatory education.

National Association of Real Estate Appraisers A professional organization certifying estate appraisers for those requiring professional appraisal reports.

National Association of Real Estate Investment Trusts (NAREIT) The national, non-profit trade organization that represents the real estate investment trust industry.

National Association of REALTORS® An organization of realtors® devoted to encouraging professionalism in real estate activities.

National Association of Review Appraisers and Mortgage Underwriters An organization that awards the Certified Review Appraiser (CRA) designation to worthy candidates.

National Council of Real Estate Investment Fiduciaries (NCREIF) A group of real estate professionals who serve on committees, sponsor research articles, seminars, and symposiums, and produce the NCREIF Property Index.

National Housing Partnership A private, for-profit company which specializes in housing for low- to moderate-income families, the handicapped, and the elderly.

Natural affection A phrase describing the feeling presumed to exist between close relatives, like a father and daughter or a husband and wife.

Natural person An individual or a private person, as opposed to an artificial entity like a corporation or partnership.

Navigable waters A body of water capable of carrying commercial vessels; sometimes called a "highway for congress."

NCREIF Property Index (NPI) A quarterly and yearly report presenting income and appreciation components.

Negative amortization An event that occurs when the deferred interest on an ARM is added, and the balance increases instead of decreases.

Negative cash flow A situation in which a property owner must make an outlay of funds to operate a property; a situation where income does not cover operating expenses.

Negative easement An easement that prevents the landowner from committing an act that would otherwise be permitted. A view easement would have the negative effect of restricting a landowner from constructing a building that would block the view in question, making it a negative easement.

Negotiable instrument A written promise or order to pay a specific sum of money that may be transferred by endorsement or delivery. The transferee then has the original payee's right to payment.

Negotiation The process of bargaining to reach an agreement. Successful negotiation results in a contract between parties.

Net after taxes Net operating income after deducting all charges, including federal and state taxes.

Net Asset Value (NAV) The total value of an asset or property minus leveraging or joint venture interests.

Net Asset Value per share The total value of a REIT's current assets divided by outstanding shares.

Net assets The total value of assets minus total liabilities based on market value.

Net cash flow The total income generated by an investment property after expenses have been subtracted.

Net income The monetary sum arrived at after deducting expenses from a business or investment but before deducting depreciation expenses.

Net investment in real estate Gross investment in properties minus the outstanding balance of debt.

Net investment income The income or loss of a portfolio or business minus all expenses, including portfolio and asset management fees, but before gains and losses on investments are considered.

Net lease A lease requiring the tenant to pay not only rent but also costs incurred in maintaining the property, including taxes, insurance, utilities, and repairs.

Net listing A listing based on the net price the seller will receive if the property is sold. Under a net listing the broker can offer the property for sale at the highest price obtainable to increase the commission. This type of listing is illegal in many states.

Net Operating Income (NOI) The pre-tax figure of gross revenue minus operating expenses and an allowance for expected vacancy.

Net Present Value (NPV) The sum of the total current value of incremental future cash flows plus the current value of estimated sales proceeds.

Net purchase price The gross purchase price minus any associated financed debt.

Net real estate investment value The total market value of all real estate minus property-level debt.

Net returns The returns paid to investors minus fees to advisers or managers.

Net sales proceeds The income from the sale of an asset, or part of an asset, minus brokerage commissions, closing costs, and market expenses.

Net spendable After-tax cash flow; the money remaining after collecting rent and paying mortgage payments and all other expenses.

Net square footage The total space usable for a task or position.

Net usable acre The portion of a property that is suitable for building, subtracting for zoning regulations, density requirements, and other building code restrictions.

Net worth The worth of an individual or company computed on the basis of the difference between all assets and liabilities.

Net yield The portion of gross yield that remains after all costs are deducted.

Never nester A couple who choose not to have children.

New town A large, mixed-use development designed to provide residences, shopping, services, and employment. The construction of a community in a previously undeveloped area under a central plan.

No cash out refinance Sometimes referred to as a rate and term refinance. A refinancing transaction which is intended only to cover the balance due on the current loan and any costs associated with obtaining the new mortgage.

No cost loan A loan for which there are no costs associated with the loan that are charged by the lender, but that typically does carry a slightly higher interest rate.

No deal-no commission clause A clause in a listing contract that stipulates a commission is to be paid if and only if and when a contract passes.

No-documentation loan A type of loan application that requires no income or asset verification; usually granted based on strong credit with a large down payment.

Nominal consideration A consideration bearing no relation to the real value of a contract, used to avoid revealing the true value of the property conveyed. Consideration in name only, with no relation to actual market value.

Nominal interest rate The stated interest rate on a note or contract, which may differ from the effective or true interest rate, especially if the lender discounts the loan.

Nominal yield The yield investors receive before it is adjusted for fees, inflation, or risk.

Nominee A person designated to act for another as a representative, but only in a limited and specified sense. A nominee corporation, for example, could purchase real estate on behalf of another person when that person wishes to remain anonymous.

Nonagent An intermediary between a buyer and seller, or landlord and tenant, who assists both parties with a transaction without representing either. Also known as a facilitator, transaction broker, transaction coordinator, or contract broker.

Nonassumption clause A provision in a loan agreement that prohibits transferring a mortgage to another borrower without approval from the lender.

Noncompete clause A provision in a lease agreement that specifies that the tenant's business is the only one that may operate in the property in question, thereby preventing a competitor moving in next door.

Nonconforming loan Any loan that is too large or does not meet certain qualifications to be purchased by Fannie Mae or Freddie Mac.

Nondiscretionary funds The funds that are allocated to an investment manager who must have approval from the investor for each transaction.

Non-Investment-Grade CMBS Also referred to as High-Yield CMBS. Commercial Mortgage Backed Securities that have ratings of BB or B.

Non liquid asset A type of asset that is not easily turned into cash. Land is considered a non liquid asset.

Nonperforming loan A loan agreement that cannot meet its contractual principal and interest payments.

Nonrecourse debt A loan that limits the lender's options to collect on the value of the real estate in the event of a default by the borrower.

Nonconforming use A use of property that is permitted to continue after a zoning ordinance prohibiting it has been established for the area.

Nondisclosure The failure to reveal a fact, with or without the intention to conceal it.

Nondisturbance clause An agreement in mortgage contracts on income producing property that provides for the continuation of leases in the event of loan foreclosure; prohibits new owners from evicting tenants who have an existing and enforceable lease.

Nonhomogenic The premise that all properties are unique, including similar houses in a tract subdivision, and that all properties carry their own bundle of rights.

Nonjudicial foreclosure The process of selling property under a power of sale in a mortgage or deed of trust that is in default. Many title insurance companies are reluctant to issue a policy unless a court has judicially foreclosed on the owner's interests.

Nonprofit corporations A corporation formed for nonprofit purposes, like a charitable, fraternal, political, or trade organization.

Nonrecourse loan A loan in which the borrower is not held personally liable in the case of default.

Nonrecurring closing costs Fees that are paid one time only for a given transaction.

Normal wear and tear Physical depreciation resulting from age and ordinary use of the property. For example, carpeting may have a physical life of five years based on normal wear and tear.

Notary public An officer who is authorized to take acknowledgements to certain types of contracts, like deeds, contracts, and mortgages, and before whom affidavits may be sworn.

Note A legal document requiring a borrower to repay a mortgage at a specified interest rate over a certain period of time.

Note rate The interest rate that is defined in a mortgage note.

Notice Official communication of a legal action, or of a person or company's intention to take an action. The announcement of a public sale is a notice. Also refers to information that may be required by the terms of a contract.

Notice of assessment The notice issued by a taxing authority specifying the assessed value of a property.

Notice of completion Legal notice filed after completion of construction.

Notice of default A formal written notification a borrower receives once the borrower is in default, stating that legal action may be taken.

Notice of dishonor A document issued by a notary public at the request of a note holder who has been refused payment of the note by its maker. The notice of dishonor is legal evidence that the note is unpaid.

Notice of nonresponsibility A legal notice designed to relieve a property owner of responsibility for the cost of improvements ordered by another person. The owner typically gives notice that he or she will not be responsible for performing the work requested.

Notice to quit A notice to a tenant to vacate rented property; can also be used by a tenant who wishes to vacate rented property on a specified date.

Novation Substituting a new obligation for an old one or substituting new parties to an existing obligation.

Nuisance A land use whose associated activities are incompatible with surrounding land uses; for example, a land use that creates offensive fumes may be incompatible with a residential neighborhood.

Null and void That which cannot be legally enforced; having no legal force, effect, or worth.

Nuncupative will An oral will declared by the testator in his or her final illness, made before witnesses and afterward reduced to writing.

Nut A slang term referring to the carrying charge on a property; the monthly expenses that must be overcome by income in order to maintain a positive cash flow.

Oath A pledge made before a notary public or other officer.

Obligation bond A bond signed by a mortgagor in excess of the loan amount; serves as a safeguard to the lender against nonpayment of taxes, insurance premiums, or any overdue interest.

Obligee The person in whose favor an obligation is entered into; one owed the obligation.

Obligor The individual or company who incurs a lawful obligation to another; a promisor.

Observed condition An appraisal method used to compare depreciation. The appraiser calculates a total depreciation amount by considering physical deterioration, functional obsolescence, and external obsolescence.

Obsolescence The loss of value due to factors that are outmoded or less useful; a loss in value due to reduced desirability and usefulness. Obsolescence may be functional or economic.

Occupancy agreement An agreement to permit the buyer to occupy the property before the close of escrow in consideration of paying the seller a specified amount of rent.

Occupancy permit A permit issued by the appropriate local governing body to establish that the property is suitable for habitation by meeting certain safety and health standards.

Occupancy rate The ratio of rented space relative to the amount of space available for rent. An apartment building with 8 out of 10 apartments rented has an occupancy rate of 80 percent.

Off record title defect A defect in title to real property that is not apparent from an examination of public records. A recorded document may not effectively transfer title if it was forged or signed by an incompetent party, for example.

Off-site costs Expenses related to construction that are spent away from the place of construction; adding a road to a subdivision is an example of an off-site cost.

Off-site management Property management functions performed away from the premises.

Off-street parking Parking spaces located on private property.

Offer A term that describes a specified price or spread to sell whole loans or securities; an expression of willingness to purchase a property at a specified price or of willingness to sell.

Offer and acceptance Two essential components of a valid contract; a "meeting of the minds;" creates an agreement of sale.

Offer to lease A document used to create an agreement for the lessor to lease commercial space to a lessee on specified terms and conditions. At closing the parties sign a formal lease agreement.

Offeror The person or company who extends the offer to another.

Office building A structure used primarily for the conduct of business relating to administration, clerical services, consulting, and other client services not related to retail sales. Office buildings can hold single or multiple firms.

Office exclusive A listing that is retained by one real estate office to the exclusion of other brokers; a listing in which the seller refuses to submit the listing to a multiple listing service (MLS).

Office of Equal Opportunity (EEO) The federal agency that administers the federal fair housing act.

Office of Interstate Land Sales Registration A division of the Department of Housing and Urban Development (HUD) that regulates land for sale across state lines.

Office of Thrift Supervision (OTS) A government agency which governs the practices of fiduciary lenders. OTS was created by the Financial Institutions Reform, Recovery, and Enforcement Act (FIRREA).

Offset statement A statement by an owner or lien holder detailing the balance due on existing liens against property being purchased.

Oil and gas lease A grant of the sole and exclusive right to explore for oil, gas, and sometimes other minerals, and to extract them from the ground.

On or before A phrase in contracts referring to the time by which a certain act must take place.

On site management Property management functions that must be performed on the premises. Showing rental units to prospective tenants is an on site function, since it must take place on the premises.

One hundred percent commission A commission arrangement between a real estate broker and a salesperson in which the salesperson receives the full net commission on certain real estate sales; typically occurs after specified quotas have been met or administrative fees have been paid to the broker.

One-year adjustable rate mortgage An ARM for which the interest rate changes annually, generally based on movements of a published index plus a specified margin.

Open and notorious possession Possession clear that a reasonable person viewing the property would know the occupant claimed some title or interest in the property. An owner does not lose property due to adverse possession unless he or she has notice of the occupant's claim to the property.

Open-end fund A type of commingled fund with an infinite life, always accepting new investor capital and making new investments in property.

Open-end loan A loan that is expandable by increments up to a maximum dollar amount, the full loan being secured by the same original mortgage.

Open house A method of showing a house for sale where the home is left open for inspection by interested parties; typically a salesperson or broker is present.

Open housing A condition under which housing units may be purchased or leased without regard for the racial, ethnic, or religious characteristics of the buyers or tenants.

Open listing A listing contract under which the broker's commission is contingent on the broker's producing a ready, willing, and able buyer before the property is sold by the seller or another broker.

Open mortgage A mortgage that has matured or is overdue, and is therefore open to foreclosure at any time.

Open space A section of land or water that has been dedicated for public or private use or enjoyment.

Operating budget A reasonable expectation of future income and expenses from property operations.

Operating cost escalation A clause that is intended to adjust rents to account for external standards such as published indexes, negotiated wage levels, or building-related expenses.

Operating expense The regular costs associated with operating and managing a property.

Operating expense ratio The mathematical relationship calculated by dividing operating expenses by potential gross income. The higher the operating expense ratio, the lower the rent must be, or the higher the operating expenses must be.

Operation of law A term that describes the way in which rights and duties belong to a person by the application of established rules of law, without any act by the person. Rights that are given by possession do not pass by contract but by law, making them subject to operation of law.

Opinion of title An opinion from an attorney, generally in certificate form, as to the validity of the title to the property being sold. Also called a title abstract.

Opportunistic A phrase that generally describes a strategy of holding investments in underperforming and/or under managed assets with the expectation of increases in cash flow and/or value.

Option An agreement to keep open for a set period an offer to sell or purchase property; frequently an option is granted for a non-refundable consideration.

Option ARM loan A type of mortgage in which the borrower has a variety of payment options each month.

Option listing Listing with a provision that gives the listing broker the right to purchase the listed property.

Option to renew A lease provision giving the tenant the right to extend the lease for an additional period of time under set terms.

Oral contract A verbal contract or unwritten agreement. Unwritten agreements for the sale or use of real estate are generally not enforceable.

Ordinance Municipal rules governing the use of land.

Ordinary and necessary business expense A tax term that allows a current deduction for business expenses. An unreasonable expense is one that is not necessary for normal business expenses.

Ordinary gain A gain or profit for which income tax must be paid at ordinary income rates. Long-term gains are taxed at a lower rate, and are, therefore, not taxed as an ordinary gain.

Orientation The position of a structure on a site relative to sunlight angles and prevailing winds. A house with a north to south orientation is designed to take advantage of the sun in winter for heating purposes.

Original principal balance The total principal owed on a mortgage before a borrower has made a payment.

Origination fee A fee that most lenders charge for the purpose of covering the costs associated with arranging the loan.

Originator A company that underwrites loans for commercial and/or multi-family properties.

Ostensible agency A form of implied agency relationship created by the actions of the parties involved rather than by written agreement or document.

Out parcel Individual retail sites located within a shopping center; a tract of land adjacent to a larger tract of which it was originally an integral part.

Outside of closing Payment of certain closing costs to someone directly, and not through the closing process itself. Noted on settlement statements as POC (paid outside closing).

Outstanding balance The amount of a loan that remains to be paid. An outstanding balance specifies an obligation.

Over allotment A practice in which the underwriters offer and sell a higher number of shares than they had planned to purchase from the issuer.

Over improvement A land use considered too intensive for the land. Building a $1,000,000 home in a neighborhood with $200,000 homes would be considered an over improvement.

Overage Amounts to be paid based on gross sales over the base rent in a lease.

Overall Rate (OAR) The direct percentage ratio between net annual operating income and sales price. The overall rate is calculated by dividing the net income by the price.

Overflow right The right to flood another person's land, either as a temporary or a permanent right.

Overhang The part of a roof that extends beyond the exterior wall.

Override A fee paid to someone higher in the organization or above a certain amount; an estate carved out of an interest in an oil and gas lease.

Overriding royalty A royalty fee retained by a lessee of an oil and gas lease when the property is subleased.

Owelty Money paid by a favored co-tenant to the other members of the tenancy where there is a physical partition of a tenancy into unequal shares. These payments are typically court ordered.

Owner financing A transaction in which the property seller agrees to finance all or part of the amount of the purchase.

Owner occupant Property owner who physically occupies the property.

Package loan A real estate loan used to finance the purchase of both real property and personal property, such as in the purchase of a new home that includes carpeting, window coverings, and major appliances.

Pad The area in a mobile home park allocated for the placement of a mobile home unit; a foundation or site suited for a specific type of improvement.

Paired sales analysis An appraisal technique used to find the value of one particular attribute. The appraiser locates two sales where the only difference is the attribute being appraised; the difference in value is considered to be the value of the attribute.

Panic peddling The illegal practice of soliciting sales or rental listings by making written or oral statements that create fear or alarm.

Paper A business term referring to a mortgage, note, or contract for deed, usually taken back from the buyer by a seller when real property is sold.

Par Average, equal, at face value. A method for comparison.

P

Paragraph 17 The mortgage provision that typically contains a due on sale clause.

Parapet The part of the wall of a house that rises above the roof line.

Parcel A specific portion of a larger tract; a lot.

Parity clause A provision that allows for a mortgage or trust deed to secure more than one note, and that provides that all notes be secured by the same mortgage without any priority or preference.

Parking ratio A figure, generally expressed as square footage, that compares a building's total rentable square footage to its total number of parking spaces.

Parol evidence rule Oral evidence, rather than evidence contained in documents. The parol evidence rule states that when parties put their agreements in writing, all previous oral agreements merge into the written agreement.

Partial eviction A situation where the landlord's negligence renders part of the premises unusable to the tenant for the purposes intended in the lease.

Partial payment An amount paid that is not large enough to cover the normal monthly payment on a mortgage loan or rental agreement.

Partial reconveyance An instrument filed when a certain portion of encumbered real estate is released from a mortgage or a trust deed.

Partial release clause A mortgage provision that allows some of the property pledged to be freed from collateral on the debt.

Partial sale The act of selling a real estate interest that is smaller than the whole property.

Partial taking The appropriating of a portion of an owner's property under the laws of eminent domain; the acquisition of only part of the property or property rights.

Partially amortized A loan that requires some payments toward principal but does not fully retire the debt, eventually requiring a balloon payment.

Participating broker A brokerage company or its sales agent who obtains a buyer for a property that is listed with another brokerage company; the participating broker normally splits the commission with the seller's broker in an agreed upon amount—usually 50 percent.

Participating debt Financing that allows the lender to have participatory rights to equity through increased income and/ or residual value over the balance of the loan or original value at the time the loan is funded.

Participation certificate A mortgage backed security sold by Freddie Mac to fund its purchases of mortgages. Participation certificates can be sold among investors similar to how bonds are sold.

Participation mortgage A mortgage loan where the lender has a partial equity interest in the property or receives a portion of the income from the property—the lender participates in the gain in equity or income from the property.

Parties Principals in a transaction or judicial proceeding. A buyer and a seller are the principals in a sales contract; a broker is not.

Partition The division of co-tenants' interests in real property when all the parties do not voluntarily agree to terminate the co-ownership; takes place through court procedures.

Partnership An association of two or more individuals who carry on a continuing business for profit as co-owners. Under the law, a partnership is regarded as a group of individuals rather than as a single entity. A general partnership is a typical form of joint venture in which each general partner shares in the administration, profits, and losses of the operation. A limited partnership is a business arrangement whereby the operation is administered by one or more general partners and funded, by and large, by limited or silent partners, who are by law responsible for losses only to the extent of their investments.

Party in interest Any party that may hold an interest, including employers, unions, and sometimes fiduciaries.

Party wall A wall that is located on or at a boundary line between two adjoining parcels of land and is used or is intended to be used by the owners of both properties.

Pass through certificate A document that allows the holder to receive payments of principal and interest from the underlying pool of mortgages.

Passive income Income from rents, royalties, dividends, interest, and gains from the sale of securities.

Passive investor An individual or company that invests money but does not manage the business or property, or contribute expertise to the venture.

Passive loss Loss from a passive activity; losses from rents, royalties, interest, and dividends.

Patent A grant or franchise of land from the U.S. government.

Payee The person to whom a debt, a check, or a promissory note is made payable; the person who is paid.

Payment bond A surety bond through which a contractor assures an owner that material and labor provided in the construction of a building will be fully paid for, and that no mechanics' liens will be filed against the owner.

Payment cap The maximum amount a monthly payment may increase on an ARM.

Payment change date The date on which a new payment amount takes effect on an ARM or GPM, usually in the month directly after the adjustment date.

Payoff The payment in full of an existing loan; the amount necessary to satisfy an outstanding debt.

Payoff statement The document signed by a lender indicating the amount required to pay a loan balance in full and satisfy the debt; used in the settlement process to protect both the seller's and the buyer's interests.

Payor The person who makes payment to another; the person who pays.

Payout ratio The percentage of the primary earnings per share, excluding unusual items, that are paid to common stockholders as cash dividends during the next 12 months.

Pedestrian traffic count A study and analysis of the number and kinds of people passing by a particular location, determining the potential buying power in a given area.

Penalty A punishment imposed for violating a law or agreement; money one will pay for breaking a law or violating part or all of the terms of a contract.

Pension liability The full amount of capital that is required to finance vested pension fund benefits.

Penthouse A luxury housing unit located on the top floor of a high rise building.

Per diem interest Interest that is charged or accrued daily.

Per unit cost method A method of computing a property management fee based on the direct cost of managing a specific number of rental units.

Percentage lease A lease, commonly used for commercial property, whose rental is based on the tenant's gross sales at the premises; it usually stipulates a base monthly rental plus a percentage of any gross sales above a certain amount.

Percentage rent The amount of rent that is adjusted based on the percentage of gross sales or revenues the tenant receives.

Percolation test A test of the soil to determine if it will absorb and drain water adequately to use a septic system for sewage disposal.

Perfect escrow An escrow in which all the documents, funds, and instructions needed to close the transaction are in the hands of the escrow agent.

Perfecting title Removing a cloud or claim against a title to real estate.

Performance The changes each quarter in fund or account values that can be explained by investment income, realized or unrealized appreciation, and the total return to the investors before and after investment management fees.

Performance based fees The fees that advisers or managers receive which are based on returns to investors.

Performance bond A bond that contractor posts to guarantee full performance of a contract in which the proceeds will be used for completing the contract or compensating the owner for loss in the event of nonperformance.

Performance measurement The process of measuring how well an investor's real estate has performed regarding individual assets, advisers/managers, and portfolios.

Periodic payment cap The highest amount that payments can increase or decrease during a given adjustment period on an ARM.

Periodic rate cap The maximum amount that the interest rate can increase or decrease during a given adjustment period on an ARM.

Periodic tenancy A leasehold estate that continues from period to period, such as month to month or year to year; the tenant has no automatic right to extend the period of tenancy.

Permanent financing A long-term loan, not a loan used for short-term purposes like a construction loan or bridge loan.

Permanent loan A long-term property mortgage.

Permissive waste The failure of lessees or life tenants to maintain and make reasonable repairs to the property under their control. Also referred to as negligent or passive waste.

Person An individual, an in some states a corporation or government agency, a business trust, a partnership, or two or more persons having a joint or common interest.

Personal property Any items belonging to a person that is not real estate; property that is movable and not fixed to land; also known as chattels.

Personal representative The title given to the person designated in a will or appointed by the probate court to settle the estate of a deceased person. Frequently known as an executor or administrator.

Petition A formal request or application to an authority, like a court, seeking specific relief or redress of some wrong. A petition can be filed requesting a zoning change, for example.

Phase I Audit An initial evaluation of a property to determine the existence of environmental problems. A Phase I audit is required to support a claim to be an innocent purchaser if environmental problems are later discovered.

Physical deterioration A reduction in a property's value resulting from a decline in physical condition; can be caused by action of the elements or by ordinary wear and tear.

Physical life The expected period of time for a real estate investment to exist physically; the actual age or life span over which a structure is considered habitable.

Pier A column placed under a structure to support its weight.

Piggyback loan A combination of a construction loan with a permanent loan commitment; one mortgage held by more than one lender, with one lender holding the rights of the others in subordination.

Pipestem lot A narrow lot, usually rectangular, that provides street or road access in heavily-developed areas. The short side of the lot is the side bordering the road. Pipestem lots are commonly found where road frontage is at a premium; also typical in beachfront or lakefront developments. Pipestem lots are also referred to as flag lots, especially when the lot creates an L-shape.

Pitch The slope of a roof or other surface; thick black substance used for repairing a driveway or street, or for repairing a roof.

PITI Principal, Interest, Taxes, Insurance. The items that are included in the monthly payment to the lender for an impounded loan, as well as mortgage insurance.

PITI reserves The amount in cash that a borrower must readily have after the down payment and all closing costs are paid when purchasing a home.

Placement fee A fee charged by a mortgage broker for negotiating a loan between the actual lender and the borrower.

Plaintiff A person who brings a lawsuit; the complainant. Opposite of a defendant.

Plan assets The assets included in a pension plan.

Plan sponsor The party that is responsible for administering an employee benefit plan.

Planned Unit Development (PUD) A type of ownership where individuals actually own the building or unit they live in, but common areas are owned jointly with the other members of the development or association. Contrast with condominium, where an individual actually owns the airspace of his unit, but the buildings and common areas are owned jointly with the others in the development or association.

Planning commission A group of citizens appointed by local government officials to conduct hearings and recommend amendments to zoning ordinances. Also called a planning board, zoning commission, or zoning board.

Plans and specifications All the drawings pertaining to a development under consideration, including the building and mechanical and electrical drawings. Includes written instructions to the builder for materials, workmanship, style, colors, and finishes.

Plant The storage facility of a title insurance company where it accumulates complete title records of properties in the area.

Plat A chart or map of a certain area showing the boundaries of individual lots, streets, and easements.

Plat book A public record of maps of subdivided land, showing the division of the land into blocks, lots, and parcels, and indicating the dimensions of individual parcels.

Plat map A map of a town, section, or subdivision indicating the location and boundaries of individual properties.

Plaza A public square or meeting place usually in the center of an area, like in the center of a shopping complex.

Pledge The transfer or delivery of property to be held as security for repayment of a debt.

Pledged Account Mortgage (PAM) A loan tied to a pledged savings account for which the fund and earned interest are used to reduce mortgage payments gradually.

Plot plan A diagram showing the proposed or existing use of a specific parcel of land. Typically shows the location, dimensions, parking areas, and landscaping.

Pocket license card Issued by the state licensing agency, it identifies its holder as a licensee and must be carried at all times.

Pocket listing A listing whose entry into the multiple listing service (MLS) is delayed until the last moment so the listing broker will have more time to find a buyer before another salesperson can find a buyer. In effect the listing is kept "in the pocket of" the listing broker.

Point Also referred to as a Discount Point. A fee a lender charges to provide a lower interest rate, equal to one percent of the amount of the loan.

Point of Beginning (POB) In a metes-and-bounds legal description, the starting point of the survey, situated in one corner of the parcel; all metes-and-bounds descriptions must follow the boundaries of the parcel back to the point of beginning.

Police power The government's right to impose laws, statutes, and ordinances, including zoning ordinances and building codes, to protect the public health, safety, and welfare.

Porte cochere A roofed structure extending from the entrance of a building over an adjacent driveway to shelter persons getting into or out of buildings.

Portfolio management Formulating, modifying, and implementing a real estate investment strategy according to an investor's investment objectives.

Portfolio turnover The amount of time averaged from the time an investment is funded until it is repaid or sold.

Positive cash flow Money remaining after collecting rent and paying operating expenses and mortgage payments. If more money is spent than earned, negative cash flow results.

Possession Holding, controlling, or having custody of property for one's use, either as an owner or as a person with a legal right.

Postdated check A check with a face date later than the actual date on which it was written. A check written on May 25 with a date of June 1 is a postdated check.

Potable water Water suitable for drinking.

Power of attorney A written instrument authorizing a person (who becomes the attorney-in-fact) to act as agent for another person to the extent indicated in the instrument.

Power of sale The clause included in a mortgage or deed of trust that provides the mortgagee (or trustee) with the right and power to advertise and sell the property at public auction if the borrower is in default.

Practice of law Rendering services specific to the legal profession.

Pre-approval The complete analysis a lender makes regarding a potential borrower's ability to pay for a home as well as a confirmation of the proposed amount to be borrowed.

Pre-approval letter The letter a lender presents which states the amount of money they are willing to lend a potential buyer.

Pre-approved loan A pending loan in which all of the underlying documents are on file and there is a strong probability that no credit or income issues will keep the loan from closing. Pre-approved loans have not necessarily passed underwriting approval, however.

Pre-qualified loan An opinion given by a lender that states that based on an examination of a credit report and an interview with a prospective borrower that borrower will qualify for a specific loan. Pre-qualification does not include a formal review of financial documents to ensure the borrower will qualify.

Preclosing A preliminary meeting before the formal closing to review documents, sign appropriate documents, and prepare for actual closing. Preclosing frequently occurs when multiple units must close in one day.

Preemption A legal doctrine that states that one law is superior to another; some federal laws preempt state laws.

Preferred shares Stocks that have a prior distributions claim up to a defined amount, before the common shareholders may receive anything.

Pre-leased A certain amount of space in a proposed building that must be leased before construction may begin or a certificate of occupancy may be issued.

Preliminary costs Costs incurred prior to actual commencement of a main cost. A feasibility study is a preliminary cost, because it is conducted before a project begins.

Preliminary report A title report made before a title insurance policy is issued. A preliminary report is not considered a title abstract; it instead states a willingness to insure the title upon closing.

Premises Land and tenements; an estate; the subject matter of a conveyance.

Premium The cost of an insurance policy; the value of a mortgage or bond in excess of its face amount; the amount over market value paid for some exceptional quality or feature.

Prepaid expenses The amount of money that is paid before it is due, including taxes, insurance, and/or assessments.

Prepaid fees The charges that a borrower must pay in advance regarding certain recurring items, such as interest, property taxes, hazard insurance, and PMI, if applicable.

Prepaid interest The amount of interest that is paid before its due date.

Prepaid items On a closing statement, items that have been paid in advance by the seller, such as insurance premiums and some real estate taxes, for which he or she must be reimbursed by the buyer.

Prepayment The money that is paid to reduce the principal balance of a loan before the date it is due.

Prepayment penalty A charge imposed on a borrower who pays off the loan principal early. This penalty compensates the lender for interest and other charges that would otherwise be lost.

Prepayment privilege The right a borrower is given to pay the total principal balance before the maturity date free of penalty; also known as a prepayment right.

Prequalification The initial assessment by a lender of a potential borrower's ability to pay for a home as well as an estimate of how much the lender is willing to supply to the buyer.

Presale Sale of proposed properties, such as condominiums or newly constructed dwellings, before actual construction begins.

Prescription Acquiring rights through adverse possession.

Present value The equivalent value of an expected future cash flow calculated according to a specific discount rate. Based on the premise that money has a time value.

Preservation district A zoning district established to protect and preserve parkland, wilderness areas, open spaces, beach reserves, scenic areas, historic areas, forestry, and grazing.

Presumption A rule of law that provides that a court will draw a particular inference from a certain fact or evidence unless or until the truth of such inference is disproved or rebutted. For example, the date of a contract is assumed to be accurate unless proven otherwise.

Prevailing party The person who wins a lawsuit.

Prevailing rate A term used to describe the average interest rate currently charged by lending institutions on mortgage loans.

Price The amount of money exchanged for something of value. Price is not value; value is an opinion of worth, whereas price is an actual amount paid that establishes value.

Price fixing An illegal effort by competing businesses to maintain a uniform price.

Price to earnings ratio The comparison that is derived by dividing the current share price by the sum of the primary earnings per share from continuing operations over the past year. Typically used as a tool to evaluate stocks.

Prima facie evidence Evidence that is good and sufficient on its face, or at face value, to establish a fact.

Primary issuance The preliminary financing of an issuer.

Primary mortgage market The mortgage market in which loans are originated and consisting of lenders such as commercial banks, savings and loan associations, and mutual savings banks.

Prime rate The lowest interest rate reserved for a bank's preferred customers for short term loans.

Prime space The first-generation space that is available for lease.

Prime tenant The major largest or highest-earning tenant in a building or shopping center.

Principal One of the main parties in a transaction; a sum loaned or employed as a fund or an investment, as distinguished from its income or profits; the original amount (as in a loan) of the total due and payable at a certain date; a main party to a transaction, or the person for whom the agent works.

Principal balance The total current balance of mortgage principal not including interest.

Principal broker The licensed broker directly in charge of and responsible for the operations conducted by the brokerage firm.

Principal meridian The main imaginary line running north and south and crossing a base line at a definite point, used by surveyors for reference in locating and describing land under the rectangular (government) survey system of legal description.

Principal paid over life of loan The final total of scheduled payments to the principal which the lender calculates to equal the face amount of the loan.

Principal payments Payments made to reduce the amount of principal in a loan.

Principal residence The place a person lives most of the time.

Principle of conformity The concept that a property will probably increase in value if its size, age, condition, and style are similar to other properties in the immediate area.

Prior appropriation A concept of water ownership in which the landowner's right to use available water is based on a government-administered permit system.

Priority The order of position or time. The priority of liens is generally determined by the chronological order in which the lien documents are recorded; tax liens, however, have priority even over previously recorded liens.

Private debt Mortgages or other liabilities for which an individual is responsible.

Private equity A real estate investment that has been acquired by a noncommercial entity.

Private Mortgage Insurance (PMI) Insurance provided by private carrier that protects a lender against a loss in the event of a foreclosure and deficiency typically required when the loan amount exceeds 80 percent of the home's value.

Private offering An offering of a real estate security that is exempt from registration with state or federal regulatory agencies because it does not involve a public offering. Typically made to a small group of investors.

Private placement The sale of a security in a way that renders it exempt from the registration rules and requirements of the SEC.

Private REIT A real estate investment company that is structured as a real estate investment trust and which places and holds shares privately rather than publicly.

Privity Mutual or successive relationship to the same rights of property; a succession in rights.

Pro forma A statement showing what is expected to occur rather than actual results.

Pro rata The proportionate amount of expenses per tenant for the property's maintenance and operation.

Probate A legal process by which a court determines who will inherit a decedent's property and what the estate's assets are.

Proceed order A written order to a general contractor to proceed with a change in contract requirements; typically subject to a later adjustment of the contract price or expected project timeline.

Proceeds of loan escrow An escrow in which loan proceeds are deposited by the lender pending the closing of a real estate transaction. Frequently used when the loan commitment is due to expire before the closing date, and the funds are held in the proceeds of loan escrow account until actual closing.

Processing fee A fee some lenders charge for gathering the information necessary to process the loan.

Procuring cause Describes effort that brings about a desired result. Under an open listing the broker who is the procuring cause of the sale receives the commission.

Production acres The portion of land that can be used directly in agriculture or timber activities to generate income, but not areas used for such things as machinery storage or support.

Profit a predre The right to take part of the soil and produce of the land — the right to take coal, fruit, or timber, for example.

Profit and loss statement A detailed breakdown of the income and expenses of a business, resulting in the operating position (or profit or loss) of a business over a specified period of time.

Progress payments Payments made as portions of a construction project are completed; construction loan funds disbursed by the lender over the course of the project instead of in one lump sum at the beginning of the project.

Progression An appraisal principle that states that, between dissimilar properties, the value of the lesser-quality property is favorably affected by the presence of the better-quality property.

Prohibited transaction Certain transactions that may not be performed between a pension plan and a party in interest, such as the following: the sale, exchange or lease of any property; a loan or other grant of credit; and furnishing goods or services.

Project Defined, for lending purposes, as a dwelling or dwellings consisting of five or more single-family units; a development like a condominium or a shopping center.

Promissory note A written agreement to repay the specific amount over a certain period of time.

Promulgate To publish or print.

Property The rights or interests an individual has in land or goods to the exclusion of all other parties; rights gained from the ownership of wealth.

Property manager Someone who manages real estate for another person for compensation. Duties include collecting rents, maintaining the property, and keeping up all accounting.

Property reports The mandatory federal and state documents compiled by sub-dividers and developers to provide potential purchasers with facts about a property, prior to their purchase.

Property residual technique An appraisal method for estimating the value of property based on estimated future income and the value of the building and land.

Property tax The tax that must be paid on private property, not on real property like real estate.

Proposition The instrument used to submit an offer, like a proposed offer to purchase.

Proprietary lease A lease given by the corporation that owns a cooperative apartment building to the shareholder for the shareholder's right as a tenant to an individual apartment.

Proprietorship Ownership of a business by an individual instead of as a partnership or a corporation.

Proration Expenses that are allocated between the seller and the buyer; expenses that are either prepaid or paid in arrears that are divided or distributed between buyer and seller at the closing.

Prospect A person considered likely to buy.

Prospectus A printed descriptive statement about a business or investment for sale to invite the interest of prospective investors.

Protected class Any group of people designated as such by the Department of Housing and Urban Development (HUD) in consideration of federal and state civil rights legislation. Currently includes ethnic minorities, women, religious groups, the handicapped, and others.

Proxy A person who represents another, usually in a meeting or in a voting situation. Also refers to the written document granting permission for one person to represent another.

Public auction An announced public meeting held at a specified location for the purpose of selling property to repay a mortgage in default.

Public debt Mortgages or other liabilities for which a commercial entity is responsible.

Public equity A real estate investment that has been acquired by REITs and other publicly traded real estate operating companies.

Public land Land owned by the federal government available for purchase by a private citizen if the land is no longer needed for government purposes.

Public offering Soliciting the general public for the sale of investment units. Typically requires the approval of the SEC or state securities agencies.

Public sale An auction sale of property with notice to the general public beforehand.

Puffing Exaggerated or superlative comments or opinions.

Punch list An itemized list that documents incomplete or unsatisfactory items after the contractor has declared the space to be mostly complete.

Punitive damages Court awarded damages to an injured party intended to punish the party found at fault. Punitive damages are not actual damages, which are damages to repay a person for actual losses suffered.

Pur autre via For the life of another. Used to refer to properties granted not in perpetuity but only for the lifespan of a specific individual.

Purchase agreement The written contract the buyer and seller both sign defining the terms and conditions under which a property is sold.

Purchase Money Mortgage (PMM) A mortgage obtained by a borrower which serves as partial payment for a property.

Purchase money transaction A transaction in which property is acquired through the exchange of money or something of equivalent value.

Purchasers policy A title insurance furnished by a seller to a purchaser under a real estate sales contract insuring the property against defects in title. Also called an owners policy.

Pyramid zoning A zoning ordinance that permits a more restricted zone classification in a less restricted zone. For instance, pyramid zoning may allow light industrial use in a heavy industrial area.

Pyramiding Acquiring additional properties by refinancing properties already owned and investing those funds in additional properties.

Quadrangle A square shaped land area, 24 miles on each side, used in the government rectangular survey method of land description.

Quadraplex A four-plex; a dwelling unit containing four separate residential units.

Quadrominium A four-unit condominium project.

Qualification Reviewing a borrower's credit and payment capacity before approving a loan.

Qualified acceptance An acceptance, in law, that amounts to a rejection of an offer and is a counteroffer; an acceptance of an offer upon certain conditions, or a qualification that has the effect of altering or modifying the terms of an offer.

Qualified buyer An individual or company who is in the market and displays some evidence of being financially able to buy a home or property within a specific price range.

Qualified plan Any employee benefit plan that the IRS has approved as a tax-exempt plan.

Qualifying ratio The measurement a lender uses to determine how much they are willing to lend to a potential buyer.

Quantity survey method The appraisal method of estimating building costs by calculating the cost of all of the physical components in the improvements, adding the cost to assemble them, and then including the indirect costs associated with such construction.

Quantum A term used to describe the amount or quantity of an estate, measuring its duration and not its quality. For example, an estate for 55 years is a quantum, not an expression of value.

Quantum meruit The legal theory under which a person can recover the reasonable value of services rendered in the absence of a legal agreement between the two parties. Also known as unjust enrichment.

Quash To annul or to set aside.

Quasi Latin term for "as if," meaning almost like or similar to. A quasi contract is a document similar to a contract.

Quick assets Assets that can be easily and quickly turned into cash; liquid assets. Real estate is not a quick asset.

Quiet title A court action to remove a cloud on the title.

Quit enjoyment The right of an owner or any other person legally entitled to possession to use a property without interference.

Quitclaim deed A written document that releases a party from any interest they may have in a property; in real estate terms, a conveyance by which the grantor transfers whatever interest he or she has in the real estate, without warranties or obligations.

Quorum The minimum number of people required to be present before a specified meeting can officially take place and authorized business can be conducted.

Radon A naturally occurring gas that is suspected of causing lung cancer.

Rafter The structural member that supports a roof.

Range A strip of land six miles wide, extending north and south and numbered east and west according to its distance from the principal meridian in the rectangular (government) survey system of legal description.

Range line Line parallel to a principal meridian marking off the land into 6-mile strips called ranges.

Range of value The market value of a property, usually stated as an amount between a high and a low limit. For example, real estate brokers often estimate a range of value for a property to help the owner determine the listing price.

Rate cap The limit on the amount the interest rate can be increased at each adjustment period in an adjustable rate loan. The cap may also set the maximum interest rate that can be charged during the life of the loan.

Rate improvement mortgage A loan that includes a clause which entitles a borrower to a one-time-only cut in the interest rate without having to refinance.

Rate lock The commitment of a lender to a borrower that guarantees a certain interest rate for a specific amount of time.

Rate of return The relationship between the annual net income of a business and the invested capital of a business. The higher the rate of return, the better the business or property produces income relative to the investment made in it.

Ratification Method of creating an agency relationship in which the principal accepts the conduct of someone who acted without prior authorization as the principal's agent.

Rating A figure that represents the credit quality or creditworthiness of securities.

Rating agencies Independent firms that are engaged to rate securities' creditworthiness on behalf of investors.

Raw land A piece of property that has not been developed and remains in its natural state.

Raw space Shell space in a building that has not yet been developed.

Ready, willing, and able buyer One who is prepared to buy property on the seller's terms and is ready to take positive steps to consummate the transaction; capable of an action, and disposed to take that action.

Real Estate Settlement Procedures Act (RESPA) The federal law that requires certain disclosures to consumers about mortgage loan settlements. The law also prohibits the payment or receipt of kickbacks and certain kinds of referral fees.

Real estate Land and everything more or less attached to it; ownership below to the center of the earth and above to the heavens; the activities concerned with ownership and transfer of physical property.

Real estate agent An individual who is licensed to negotiate and transact the real estate sales.

Real estate fundamentals The factors that drive the value of property.

Real Estate Investment Trust (REIT) Trust ownership of real estate by a group of individuals who purchase certificates of ownership in the trust, which in turn invests the money in real property and distributes the profits back to the investors free of corporate income tax.

Real estate license law State law enacted to protect the public from fraud, dishonesty, and incompetence in the purchase and sale of real estate.

Real Estate Mortgage Investment Conduit (REMIC) An investment vehicle that is designed to hold a pool of mortgages solely to issue multiple classes of mortgage-backed securities in a way that avoids doubled corporate tax.

Real Estate Mortgage Trust (REMT) A REIT that buys and sells real estate mortgages (usually short-term junior instruments) rather than real property. Sources of income for REMTs are interest, origination fees, and profits earned from buying and selling mortgages.

Real Estate Owned (REO) The real estate that a savings institution owns as a result of foreclosure on borrowers in default; properties that did not sell at foreclosure auction and have reverted to ownership by the lender.

Real estate recovery fund A fund established in some states from real estate license revenues to cover claims of aggrieved parties who have suffered monetary damage through the actions of a real estate licensee.

Real Estate Settlement Procedures Act (RESPA) A legislation for consumer protection that requires lenders to notify borrowers regarding closing costs in advance.

Real property The interests, benefits, and rights inherent in real estate ownership; land and anything else of a permanent nature that is affixed to the land.

Real rate of return The yield given to investors minus an inflationary factor.

Realized gain A gain that has occurred financially but is not necessarily taxed; the profit made from the sale of a capital asset — usually the difference between the net sales price and the adjusted tax basis of the property.

Realtist A member of a national organization known as the National Association of Real Estate Brokers (NAREB).

REALTOR® A registered trademark term reserved for the sole use of active members of local REALTOR® boards affiliated with the National Association of REALTORS®.

Realty Land and everything more or less attached to it; ownership below to the center of the earth and above to the heavens; the activities concerned with ownership and transfer of physical property.

Reappraisal lease A lease where the rental level is periodically reviewed by independent appraisers. Often the lessor and lessee will each select an appraiser, and if they do not agree on a value, they will select a third appraiser.

Reasonable time A fair length of time that may be allowed or required for an act to be completed considering the nature of the act and the surrounding circumstances. Contracts that do not include reasonable time frames for the completion of acts are often challengeable in court.

Rebate A refund resulting from a purchase or tax; a kickback or charge, often illegal if done without the knowledge of all parties.

Recapture The act of the IRS recovering the tax benefit of a deduction or a credit that a taxpayer has previously taken in error.

Recapture clause A clause in a contract permitting the party who grants an interest or right to take it back under certain conditions. A recapture clause may also be used to give a ground lessee the right to purchase the fee after a set period of time has elapsed.

Recapture rate A term used in appraisals to describe the rate of recovery of an investment.

Recasting The process of redesigning existing loans, especially under the threat of default. The term of the loan may be extended or the interest rate adjusted to lessen the financial pressure on the borrower.

Receipt A written acknowledgement of having received money, goods, or services.

Receiver An independent party assigned by a court to receive, preserve, and manage property involved in litigation pending final disposition of the matter before the court.

Reciprocal easements Easements and restrictions limiting the use of the land for the benefit of all owners in a subdivision or development; easements that apply to all involved.

Reciprocity Mutual agreement to accept; mutual exchanges of privileges.

Recital A statement defining the consideration involved in a transaction. For example, a deed does not require consideration for title to be passed, but most experts recommend reciting consideration, especially to support any covenants, restrictions, or promises made in the deed itself. Frequently the consideration recited is not the actual consideration eventually offered; the words "for good and valuable consideration" frequently appear as a recital statement.

Reclamation Causing a change in land from an unusable or undevelopable state to a developable state; converting wasted natural resources into productive assets. Draining swampland would be considered reclamation.

Recognition A tax term meaning that a transaction is a taxable event.

Recognition clause A clause found in some mortgages and contracts providing for the protection of the rights of the ultimate buyers of individual lots in case of default of the blanket mortgage of the developer.

Reconciliation The final step in the appraisal process, in which the appraiser combines the estimates of value received from the sales comparison, cost, and income approaches to arrive at a final estimate of market value for the subject property.

Reconveyance An event that occurs when a mortgage debt is retired—the lender conveys the ownership back to the borrower, free of the debt.

Record owner The owner of record; the owner of the property as shown by an examination of the records; the individual or company having recorded title.

Record title Title as it appears from an examination of public records; the title on record.

Recording The act of entering or recording documents affecting or conveying interests in real estate in the recorder's office established in each county. Until it is recorded, a deed or mortgage ordinarily is not effective against subsequent purchasers or mortgagees; the documentation that the registrar's office keeps of the details of properly executed legal documents.

Recording fee A fee real estate agents charge for moving the sale of a piece of property into the public record.

Recourse The option a lender has for recovering losses against the personal assets of a secondary party who is also liable for a debt that is in default.

Recourse note A debt instrument a lender can use to take action against the borrower or endorser personally, in addition to foreclosure of the property covering the lender's mortgage.

Recovery fund Maintained by the Real Estate Commission, a fund licensees contribute to and used to reimburse aggrieved persons who are unable to collect from brokers for wrongdoing.

Recreational lease A contract in which the lessor leases recreational facilities to a tenant for rent considerations. Typically offered by developers of large subdivisions that include swimming pools, tennis courts, or other recreational facilities constructed by the developer but for use by the residents.

Rectangular (government) survey system A system established in 1785 by the federal government, providing for surveying and describing land by reference to principal meridians and base lines.

Red herring An early prospectus that is distributed to prospective investors that includes a note in red ink on the cover stating that the SEC-approved registration statement is not yet in effect.

Reddendum clause A clause in a conveyance that reserves something for the grantor.

Redemption The right of a defaulted property owner to recover his or her property by curing the default.

Redemption period A period of time established by state law during which a property owner has the right to redeem his or her real estate from a foreclosure or tax sale by paying the sales price, interest, and costs. Many states do not have mortgage redemption laws.

Redemption, equitable right of The right of the mortgagee to redeem or get back title to a property he or she has defaulted on before the foreclosure sale actually takes place. Requires the mortgagee to pay back payments and bring the mortgage current.

Rediscount rate The rate of interest charged to member banks when they borrow from the Federal Reserve System. Frequently called the discount rate.

Redlining An illegal practice of a lender who refuses to make home loans in certain areas, regardless of the qualifications of prospective borrowers.

Reduction certificate The document signed by a lender indicating the amount required to pay a loan balance in full and satisfy the debt; used in the settlement process to protect both the seller's and the buyer's interests. Also referred to as a payoff statement.

Reentry The legal right of a landlord to possess the property when the term for possession by the tenant has expired.

Referee A neutral third party appointed by the court to arbitrate, investigate, find facts, or settle a dispute or legal matter.

Referral agency A brokerage company where licensed salespeople agree to obtain leads only on prospective buyers and sellers; no other real estate services are permitted. The referral agency then receives a fee on sale from the agency referred to.

Refinance To replace an old loan with a new loan; to pay off one loan with the proceeds from another loan.

Refinance transaction The act of paying off an existing loan using the funding gained from a new loan which uses the same property as security.

Reformation A legal action to correct or modify a deed that has not accurately reflected the intentions of the parties due to some error—typically a typographical error in the contract.

Regional diversification Boundaries that are defined based on geography or economic lines.

Regional shipping center A large shopping center containing from 70 to 225 stores and between 300,000 and 900,000 square feet of shopping space.

Registered land Land that is registered in the Torrens system.

Registrar The person who maintains accurate and official records like deeds, mortgages, and other recorded documents.

Registration statement The set of forms that are filed with the SEC (or the appropriate state agency) regarding a proposed offering of new securities or the listing of outstanding securities on a national exchange.

Regression An appraisal principle that states that, between dissimilar properties, the value of the better-quality property is affected adversely by the presence of the lesser-quality property.

Regulation A rule or order prescribed for management or government. Regulations frequently have the force and effect of law.

Regulation Z A federal legislation under the Truth in Lending Act that requires lenders to advise the borrower in writing of all costs that are associated with the credit portion of a financial transaction.

Rehab Short for Rehabilitation. Refers to an extensive renovation intended to extend the life of a building or project.

Rehabilitate To restore a structure to the condition of good repair.

Rehabilitation mortgage A loan meant to fund the repairing and improving of a resale home or building.

Reinstatement To bring something back to its prior position. A defaulted loan that is returned to paid-up status is considered a reinstatement.

Reinsurance A contract by which the original insurer obtains insurance from another insurance covering against loss on the original policy. The reinsurance company assumes the rights, duties, and liabilities of the original insurer.

Reissue rate A reduced charge by a title insurance company for a new policy if a previous policy on the same property was recently issued.

REIT A Real Estate Investment Trust or REIT (rhymes with treat) is a tax designation for a corporation investing in real estate that reduces or eliminates corporate income taxes. The REIT structure was designed to provide a similar structure for investment in real estate as mutual funds provide for investment in stocks.

Related parties Parties in a certain defined relationship to each other, either by blood, by ownership interests, or by fiduciary relationship. Related parties are subject to different tax treatment on the gain or loss of investments exchanged, for example.

Release To free real estate from a mortgage; also known as a release of lien.

Release clause A clause in a mortgage that gives the owner the privilege of paying off a portion of the mortgage indebtedness, thus freeing a portion of the property from the mortgage.

Release deed A document also known as a deed of reconveyance that transfers all rights given a trustee under a deed of trust loan back to the grantor after the loan has been fully repaid.

Reliction Gradual subsiding of waters that leaves dry land.

Relinquished property The first property transferred in a delayed tax-deferred exchange. The property for which the exchange is made is called the replacement property.

Relocation clause A lease stipulation that allows the landlord to move the tenant to another dwelling within the building.

Relocation company A company that contracts with other firms to arrange the relocation of an employee from one city to another. Typically handles the sale of a home and the purchase of a new home, along with other moving-related services.

Remainder interest The remnant of an estate that has been conveyed to take effect and be enjoyed after the termination of a prior estate, such as when an owner conveys a life estate to one party and the remainder to another.

Remaining balance The amount of the principal on a home loan that has not yet been paid.

Remaining term The original term of the loan after the number of payments made has been subtracted; the number of payments or time period left on a loan.

Remediation Corrective action to clean up an environmentally contaminated site or to reduce the contamination to an acceptable level.

Rendering Drawing or painting showing a perspective view of a prospective development to show how it will look when completed; typically an artistic view rather than a merely technical view of the proposed development or property.

Renegotiable Rate Mortgage (RRM) A loan whose interest rate is revised at specific intervals; those revisions are not tied to an index, however.

Renegotiation of lease The review of an existing lease at a specific time to negotiate new lease terms.

Renewal option A clause in a lease agreement that allows a tenant to extend the term of a lease.

Renewal probability The average percentage of a building's tenants who are expected to renew terms at market rental rates upon the lease expiration.

Rent The fee paid for the occupancy and/or use of any rental property or equipment.

Rent commencement date The date on which a tenant is to begin paying rent.

Rent control Regulations by state or local governments restricting the amount of rent landlords can charge tenants; designed to keep the cost of housing affordable for residents.

Rent escalation Adjustment of rent by the landlord to cover changes in cost of living or for property maintenance costs.

Rent loss insurance A policy that covers loss of rent or rental value for a landlord due to any condition that renders the leased premises inhabitable, thereby excusing the tenant from paying rent.

Rent roll A list of tenants showing the lease rent and the expiration rate for each tenant.

Rent schedule A statement of proposed rental rates, determined by the owner or the property manager or both, based on a building's estimated expenses, market supply and demand, and the owner's long-range goals for the property.

Rent up period The period of time following completion of a new building when tenants are actively being sought and the project is stabilizing.

Rentable to usable ratio The total rentable area in a building divided by the area available for use.

Rental agency A person who is compensated or receives consideration to act as an intermediary between a landlord and a prospective tenant.

Rental agreement A written or oral agreement that establishes or modifies the terms and conditions concerning the use and occupancy of a dwelling and its premises.

Rental growth rate The projected trend of market rental rates over a particular period of analysis.

Repairs Work performed to restore a property to a former condition without extending its useful life. An improvement is not a repair. Repairs are operating expenses, not capital expenses.

Repayment plan An agreement made to repay late installments or advances.

Replacement cost The projected cost by current standards of constructing a building that is equivalent to the building being appraised.

Replacement property The property exchanged in a tax-deferred exchange.

Replacement reserve fund Money that is set aside for replacing of common property in a condominium, PUD, or cooperative project.

Replevin Legal proceedings to recover possession of personal property unlawfully taken, such as when a landlord has unlawfully taken the personal belongs of the tenant due to the tenant's failure to pay rent.

Reproduction cost The construction cost at current prices of an exact duplicate of the subject property.

Request for Proposal (RFP) A formal request that invites investment managers to submit information regarding investment strategies, historical investment performance, current investment opportunities, investment management fees, and other pension fund client relationships used by their firm.

Rescission The practice of one party's canceling or terminating a contract, which has the effect of returning the parties to their original positions before the contract was made.

Rescission clause A specific clause occasionally found in contracts for deed that require the seller to return all the buyer's payments, minus a fair rental value, if the buyer defaults.

Reserve account An account that must be funded by the borrower to protect the lender.

Reserve for replacements An amount set aside for the possibility of economic setback or for the replacement of worn out assets; an allowance that is necessary to maintain a projected level of income.

Reserve fund An account maintained to provide funds for anticipated expenditures to maintain a building. Reserve funds are typically held in escrow.

Residence The place where one lives, particularly the dwelling where one lives.

Residence property Raw land or improved property with buildings designed for human occupation.

Resident manager Individual who supervises the care of an apartment complex while living in one of the units in the complex.

Residual process An appraisal process used in the income approach to estimate the value of the land and buildings as indicated by the capitalization of the net income attributable to it.

Resolution Trust Corporation (RTC) The congressional corporation established for the purpose of containing, managing, and selling failed financial institutions, thereby recovering taxpayer funds.

Resort property Property that lends itself to vacationers, recreation, or leisure activity because of its natural resources or beauty, or its improvements. Beaches, lakes, golf courses, and ski resorts are all considered resort properties.

Respondeat superior The doctrine that a principal is liable for the acts of an agent if those acts were performed within the scope of the agent's authority.

Restraint of trade Contracts that are designed to eliminate or stifle competition, to create a monopoly, to control prices, or to otherwise hinder competing business activity. Restraint of trade is typically illegal if proven.

Restraint on alienation A limit on the right to transfer property. If the condition is unreasonable, the courts will void the condition.

Restriction A limitation placed on the use of property, contained in the deed or other written instrument, or in local ordinances.

Restrictive covenant A clause in a deed that limits the way the real estate ownership may be used.

Resubdivision Taking an existing subdivision and dividing it even further into additional lots.

Retail investor An investor who sells interests directly to consumers.

Retainage Money earned by a contractor but not paid to the contractor until the completion of construction or at other agreed-upon stages or dates.

Retaining wall A vertical partition used to restrict the movement of soil or water.

Retaliatory eviction The requirement by a landlord that a tenant vacate a unit in response to a complaint from the tenant concerning the condition of the building. Typically illegal if proper channels are taken to forward the complaint.

Retention rate The percentage of trailing year's earnings that have been dispersed into the company again. It is calculated as 100 minus the trailing 12-month payout ratio.

Retroactive liability Liability is not limited to the current owner, but includes people who have owned the site in the past.

Return on Assets (ROA) The measurement of the ability to produce net profits efficiently by making use of assets.

Return on Equity (ROE) The measurement of the return on the investment in a business or property.

Return on Investments (ROI) The percentage of money that has been gained as a result of certain investments.

Revenue Per Available Room (RevPAR) The total room revenue for a particular period divided by the average number of rooms available in a hospitality facility.

Revenue stamp Stamps affixed to deeds and other documents to indicate the payment of the state's transfer tax.

Reverse Annuity Mortgage (RAM) A loan under which the homeowner receives monthly payments based on his or her accumulated equity rather than a lump sum. The loan must be repaid at a prearranged date, or upon the death of the owner, or upon the sale of the property.

Reverse leverage The situation that occurs when the total yield on a cash investment is less than the interest rate on borrowed funds — indicates that financing is too costly.

Reverse mortgage A type of mortgage designed for persons with substantial equity where the lender makes periodic payments to the borrower; the payments are taken from the equity in the property.

Reversion The right of a lessor to possess leased property upon the termination of a lease.

Reversion capitalization rate The capitalization rate that is used to derive reversion value.

Reversion value A benefit that an investor expects to receive as a lump sum at the end of an investment.

Reversionary factor The mathematical factor that indicates the present worth of one dollar to be received in the future. Typically used to determine the current value of a reversion.

Reversionary interest The remnant of an estate that the grantor holds after granting a life estate to another person.

Reversionary right The return of the rights of possession and quiet enjoyment to the lessor at the expiration of a lease.

Review appraiser An appraiser who specializes in appraisal reviews. Typically a review appraiser works for a bank or the government.

Revocation An act of recalling a power of authority conferred. Recalling a power of attorney, for example, is considered the revocation a power of attorney.

Revolving debt A credit arrangement which enables a customer to borrow against a predetermined line of credit when purchasing goods and services.

Rider An amendment or attachment to a contract; an addendum.

Right of contribution The right of an individual who has discharged a common liability to recover from another liable party his or her share.

Right of first refusal A lease clause that gives a tenant the first opportunity to buy a property or to lease additional space in a property at the same price and terms as those contained in an offer from a third-party that the owner has expressed a willingness to accept.

Right of ingress or egress The option to enter or to leave the premises in question.

Right of survivorship The option that survivors have to take on the interest of a deceased joint tenant.

Right of way The right given by one landowner to another to pass over the land, construct a roadway, or use as a pathway, without actually transferring ownership.

Right to rescission A legal provision that enables borrowers to cancel certain loan types within three days after they sign.

Right to use The legal right to use or occupy a property.

Riparian lease An agreement covering the leasing of lands situated between the high water mark and the low water mark.

Riparian rights An owner's rights in land that borders on or includes a stream, river, or lake. These rights include access to and use of the water.

Risk adjusted rate of return A percentage that is used to identify investment options that are expected to deliver a positive premium despite their volatility.

Risk management A logical approach to analyzing and defining insurable and non-insurable risks while evaluating the availability and costs of purchasing third-party insurance.

Road show A tour of the executives of a company that is planning to go public, during which the executives travel to a variety of cities to make presentations to underwriters and analysts regarding their company and IPO.

Rod A linear unit of measurement equal to 16.5 feet.

Roll over risk The possibility that tenants will not renew their lease.

Rollover Tax provisions that enable a taxpayer to defer paying taxes in certain situations, such as in an exchange of real property or involuntary conversion.

Roof inspection clause A clause sometimes inserted in real estate contracts stating that the seller must supply a report of the kind and condition of a structure's roof. If the roof is found to be faulty or in disrepair, it must be repaired at the seller's expense.

Rooming house A house where bedrooms are furnished to paying guests; can, but does not have to, assume kitchen privileges are granted.

Row house Single family dwelling units attached to each other by common walls, usually with a common façade.

Royalty Money paid to a property owner for the extraction of a valuable resource from the land.

Rule of 72s A mathematical equation that will approximate the amount of time it will take a sum of money to double when earning compound interest. Dividing the percentage rate earned into 72 yields the number of years it will take for the original sum to double in value.

Rule of five A rule of thumb subdividers use to estimate subdivision costs. In general, 20 percent of the final total sales price will be allocated to land acquisition; 20 percent of the total sales price to improvement costs like grading, road installation; 20 percent to miscellaneous costs like interest, carrying charges, and unsold lots; and 40 percent to administrative costs, sales commissions, and profits.

Rules and regulations Real estate licensing authority orders that govern licensees' activities; they usually have the same force and effect as statutory law.

Run with the land An expression indicating a right or restriction that affects all current and future owners of a property; the right "runs with the land."

Rural An area outside large and moderate-sized cities and their surrounding population concentrations.

R-value A measure of the heat conductivity of a material; used to designate the insulation quality of building materials.

Sale and leaseback A transaction in which an owner sells his or her improved property and, as part of the same transaction, signs a long-term lease to remain in possession of the premises.

Sale of leased property The owner of property who has given a lease to one person may sell the leased property to another, but the new owner takes the property subject to the existing lease.

Sales assessment ratio The ratio of the assessed value of a property to its selling price. A property with an assessed value of $80,000 that sells for $100,000 has a sales assessment ratio of 80 percent.

Sales associate Licensed salesperson or broker who works for a broker.

Sales comparison approach The process of estimating the value of a property by examining and comparing actual sales of comparable properties.

Sales comparison value A value that is calculated by comparing the appraised property to similar properties in the area that have been recently sold.

Sales contract An agreement that both the buyer and seller sign defining the terms of a property sale.

Salesperson A person who performs real estate activities while employed by or associated with a licensed real estate broker.

Salvage value The estimated value an asset will have at the end of its useful life.

Satellite city A planned city in the natural growth path of a nearby larger city designed to stop urban sprawl to the suburbs and to supplement and aid the larger city's expansion.

Satellite tenant Tenants in a shopping center or mall other than the anchor tenants.

Satisfaction The payment of a debt or obligation.

Satisfaction of mortgage A document acknowledging the payment of a mortgage debt.

Savings and Loan Association (S & L) Depository institution that specializes in originating, servicing, and holding mortgage loans, primarily on residential properties.

Scarcity A lack of supply of some commodity or item; in real estate terms, the scarcity of available properties (supply) tends to lead to an increase in prices if the number of buyers is high (demand).

Scenic easement An encumbrance on a title to preserve it in a natural or undeveloped state.

Schematics Preliminary architectural drawings and sketches created at the planning stage of a project; basic layouts not containing final details.

Scope of authority A rule of law stating that a principal is liable to third parties for all wrongful acts committed by his or her agents while transacting the principal's business, whether the principal authorized the act.

Sealed and delivered A phrase indicating that a transferor has received adequate compensation based on his or her voluntary delivery.

Seasoned loan A loan on which several payments have been received or collected.

Second generation leasing Leasing of space in buildings already constructed and previously occupied by other tenants. The term is typically used in the shopping center industry.

Second mortgage A secondary loan obtained upon a piece of property; a subordinated lien created over a mortgage loan.

Secondary (follow on) offering An offering of stock made by a company that is already public.

Secondary financing A junior mortgage placed on property to help finance the purchase price. Most government loan programs, like FHA or VA loans, permit secondary financing with certain restrictions.

Secondary market A market in which existing mortgages are bought and sold as part of a mortgages pool; a market for the purchase and sale of existing mortgages, designed to provide greater liquidity for mortgages; also called the secondary money market. Mortgages are first originated in the primary mortgage market.

Secondary space Space that has been occupied before and becomes available for lease again, either by the landlord or as a sublease.

Section A portion of township under the rectangular (government) survey system. A township is divided into 36 sections, numbered 1 through 36. A section is a square with mile-long sides and an area of one square mile, or 640 acres.

Section 8 housing Privately owned rental dwelling units participating in the government's low income rental housing assistance program. The Department of Housing and Urban Development pays a portion of the fair market rent value, with the tenant paying the other portion.

Secured loan A loan that is secured by some sort of collateral.

Secured party The person having the security interest; the mortgagee or pledgee is the secured party.

Securities and Exchange Commission (SEC) The federal agency that oversees the issuing and exchanging of public securities.

Securitization The act of converting a non-liquid asset into a tradable form.

Security The property or other asset that will server as a loan's collateral.

Security agreement See Uniform Commercial Code.

Security deposit A payment by a tenant, held by the landlord during the lease term, and kept (wholly or partially) on default, or on destruction of the premises by the tenant.

Seisen The ownership of real property under a claim of freehold estate.

Seizing Taking of property by the government when the property is being used to conduct an illegal act.

Self-administered REIT A REIT in which the management are employees of the REIT or similar entity.

Self help The efforts of a landlord to cure a default on a lease without legal proceedings. Self help remedies are typically not considered a legitimate substitute for a legal eviction.

Self managed REIT A REIT in which the management are employees of the REIT or similar entity.

Seller carry back An arrangement in which the seller provides some or all of the financing to purchase a home.

Seller financing A debt instrument taken by the seller to provide financing to a buyer.

Seller's market Economic conditions that favor sellers, due to circumstances like a scarcity of supply or excessive demand.

Selling broker The licensed real estate broker that finds or brings forth the buyer.

Semi-detached dwelling A residence that shares one wall with an adjoining building, sometimes called a party wall.

Senior classes The security classes who have the highest priority for receiving payments from the underlying mortgage loans.

Separate account A relationship in which a single pension plan sponsor is used to retain an investment manager under a stated investment policy exclusively for that sponsor.

Separate property Under community property law, property owned solely by either spouse before marriage, acquired by gift or inheritance after marriage, or purchased with separate funds after marriage.

Sequestrate order A writ authorizing the taking of land, rents, and profits owed by a defendant in a concluded suit for the purpose of forcing the defendant to comply with a court order.

Service of process The legal act of notifying the defendant of an impending lawsuit, and the delivery to him or her of the summons or complaint in the action. An individual who receives said documents is considered to have been served.

Servicer An organization that collects principal and interest payments from borrowers and manages borrowers' escrow accounts on behalf of a trustee.

Servicing The process of collecting mortgage payments from borrowers as well as related responsibilities.

Servitude A burden or charge on an estate.

Set aside letter A letter from a lender to a contractor of a project stating that the lender will set aside money for the contractor, inducing the contractor to finish a project.

Setback The amount of space local zoning regulations require between a lot line and a building line; the distance required from a given reference point before a structure can be built.

Setoff The claim a debtor can make against a creditor that reduces or cancels the amount the debtor owes.

Settlement The same as closing; the act of adjusting and prorating the credits and charges to conclude a real estate transaction.

Settlement or closing fees Fees that the escrow agent receives for carrying out the written instructions in the agreement between borrower and lender and/or buyer and seller.

Settlement statement Same as a closing statement; a detailed cash accounting of a real estate transaction showing all cash received, all charges and credits made, and all cash paid out as a result of the transaction.

Severalty Ownership of real property by one person only, also called sole ownership.

Severance Changing an item of real estate to personal property by detaching it from the land; for example, cutting a tree.

Severance damages Value arising out of a condemnation to which a tract was a part.

Shall That which is required by law.

Sharecropping In an agricultural lease, the agreement between the landowner and the tenant farmer to split the crop or the profit from its sale, actually sharing the crop.

Shared Appreciation Mortgage (SAM) A mortgage loan in which the lender, in exchange for a loan with a favorable interest rate, participates in the profits (if any) the borrower receives when the property is eventually sold.

Shared equity transaction A transaction in which two people purchase a property, one to use as a residence and the other as an investment.

Shares outstanding The number of shares of outstanding common stock minus the treasury shares.

Shell lease A lease in which a tenant leases the unfinished shell of a building and agrees to complete construction.

Sheriffs deed Deed given by a court to effect the sale of property to satisfy a judgment.

Shopping center A collection of retail stores with a common parking area, usually containing a combination of department stores, grocery stores, and retail and food stores.

Shoreline The dividing line between private land and public beach on a beachfront property.

Shoring The use of timbers to prevent the sliding of earth adjoining an excavation.

Short form document A brief document that refers to a contract and restates the fact that a contract has been made between two or more parties.

Short rate A higher periodic rate charged for a shorter term than what was originally contracted for; the increased rate charged by an insurance company upon early cancellation of a policy.

Short sale A sale of secured real property that results in less money than is owed the lender. The lender releases its mortgage so the property can be sold free and clear to the new purchaser. By doing so, the lender has cut its losses by agreeing to a short sale instead of initiating the foreclosure process.

Short-term capital gain Gain on the sale of a capital asset held for less than 12 months. Short term gains are typically taxed at a higher rate than long term gains.

Should Legal language meaning recommended but not required by law.

Sick building syndrome A phrase used to describe indoor air quality problems in commercial and industrial problems that lead to headaches, nausea, and skin and eye irritations.

Sight line A view plane; a direction of view along a specific orientation or plane.

Signage Signs; in legal documents usually refers to whether signs are allowed, and what restrictions may be in place regarding the number, size, and type of sign allowed.

Signature Use of a handwritten name on an instrument to signify acceptance.

Silent partner An inactive partner in a business; a partner who has an investment interest but offers no advice, counsel, or input.

Silent second An unrecorded second mortgage, typically kept secret from the underlying first mortgage.

Simple interest A method of calculating the future value of a sum assuming that interest paid is not compounded – interest is only paid on the principal, not on unpaid interest.

Single family residence A residential structure designed to include one dwelling, or to house one family; a private home.

Sinking fund A fund created to gradually collect enough money to satisfy a debt or meet a specific requirement or expense.

Site A plot of land prepared for or underlying a structure or development; the location of a property.

Site analysis A determination of how suitable a specific parcel of land is for a particular use.

Site development The implementation of all improvements that are needed for a site before construction may begin.

Site office A temporary administrative facility where business relating to a specific property is conducted.

Site plan A detailed description and map of the location of improvements to a parcel.

Situs The economic attributes of a location, including the relationship between the property and surrounding properties. Situs is the aspect of location that contributes to a property's market value.

Sky lease A lease of air rights above a property.

Slab The flat, exposed surface that is laid over the structural support beams to form the building's floor(s).

Slander of title A civil wrong where a person maliciously makes negative statements about another individual's title to a property that then causes injury to that party.

Sleeper note A promissory note where the interest and principal are payable together on a future date.

Slum clearance The clearing of old decrepit buildings to allow the land to be put to a better and more productive use. Also frequently referred to as urban renewal.

Small claims court A court where claims of typically less than $1,000 are adjudicated; provides a relatively inexpensive forum for the disposition of minor controversies or disagreements.

Social investing A strategy in which investments are driven in partially or completely by social or non-real estate objectives.

Society of Industrial and Office REALTORS® (SIOR) An organization whose members focus on the sale of warehouses, factories, and other industrial properties. Members carry the SIOR designation.

Society of Real Estate Appraisers (SREA) An international organization of professional real estate appraisers.

Soft cost The part of an equity investment, aside from the literal cost of the improvements, that could be tax-deductible in the first year.

Soft money Money contributed to a development or investment that is tax deductible; a term used to describe costs that do not physically go into construction, like interest during construction, legal fees, and architectural fees.

Soil bank Land held out of agricultural production in an attempt to stabilize commodity prices by decreasing supply, and to promote soil conservation.

Solar easement An easement protecting an owner's access to light and to the rays of the sun. The easement creates a right to light on the owner's property, a right which is not otherwise guaranteed.

Solar heating A natural system of heating using the energy of the sun to provide heat to the household or to heat water.

Sole proprietorship Ownership of a business with no formal entity created as a business structure; a business owner with no partners.

Space plan A chart or map of space requirements for a tenant which include wall/door locations, room sizes, and even furniture layouts.

Spec home A single family dwelling constructed in anticipation of finding a buyer. A spec home is built by a contractor in hopes of finding a buyer, and not due to a contract already reached with a buyer to build the home.

Special agent One who is authorized by a principal to perform a single act or transaction; a real estate broker is usually a special agent authorized to find a ready, willing, and able buyer for a particular property.

Special assessment A tax or levy customarily imposed against only those specific parcels of real estate that will benefit from a proposed public improvement like a street or sewer.

Special benefit Benefits affecting the untaken portion of property in a partial condemnation that are to the advantage of the owner or increase the value of the untaken property. The value of special benefits can reduce a condemnation award to the owner.

Special conditions Specific conditions in a real estate contract that must be satisfied before a contract is considered binding. Frequently referred to as contingencies.

Special lien A lien or charge against a specific parcel or portion of a property; contrasts with a general lien, which is a charge against all property of the debtor.

Special purpose property A building with limited uses and marketability, like a school, theater, or church.

Special servicer A company that is hired to collect on mortgages that are either delinquent or in default.

Special use permit A right granted by a zoning authority to conduct certain activities not normally allowed within the zoning district. Also called a conditional use permit.

Special warranty deed A deed in which the grantor warrants, or guarantees, the title only against defects arising during the period of his or her tenure and ownership of the property and not against defects existing before that time, generally using the language, "by, through, or under the grantor but not otherwise."

Specific lien A lien affecting or attaching only to a certain, specific parcel of land or piece of property.

Specific performance A legal action to compel a party to carry out the terms of a contract.

Specifications Detailed instructions provided in conjunction with plans and blueprints for construction. Specifications frequently describe the materials to be used, dimensions, colors, or construction techniques.

Specified investing A strategy of investment in individually specified properties, portfolios, or commingled funds are fully or partially detailed prior to the commitment of investor capital.

Speculation An investment or other decision whose success depends on an event or change that is not certain to occur. A developer may purchase land for a higher than market price based on his or her speculation that a zoning change will take place that will increase the value of the property.

Speculative space Any space in a rental property that has not been leased prior to the beginning of construction on a new building.

Spin off The transfer of company assets to a recently formed subsidiary.

Spite fence A fence that is erected of a height or type designed to annoy a neighbor. Some states have statutes restricting the height of a fence to avoid the spite fence situation.

Split fee financing A form of joint venture in which the lender purchases the land and leases it to the developer. The lender also finances the improvements to the land.

Split level A home with a one-story wing constructed beside or between the levels of a two-story wing.

Split rate Capitalization rates applied separately to land and improvements; used to determine the value of each separately instead of as a whole.

Splitting fees Sharing compensation. In real estate terms, a broker can generally only split a commission with the buyer or seller or with another licensed real estate salesperson.

Spot loan A loan on a particular property (usually a condominium) by a lender who has not previously financed that particular condominium project. Many lenders are unwilling to lend money for a single unit in a large condominium development unless they receive special fees for legal fees and other services.

Spot zoning Rezoning a parcel of land where all surrounding parcels are zoned for a different use. Spot zoning is usually disallowed in courts.

Spreading agreement An agreement that extends the collateral of a loan to include several properties. It in effect creates second liens on other properties owned by the borrower.

Square Area measuring 24 miles by 24 miles. Also called quadrangle.

Square foot method The appraisal method of estimating building costs by multiplying the number of square feet in the improvements being appraised by the cost per square foot for recently constructed similar improvements.

Stabilized net operating income Expected income minus expenses that reflect relatively stable operations.

Stabilized occupancy The best projected range of long-term occupancy that a piece of rental property will achieve after existing in the open market for a reasonable period of time with terms and conditions that are comparable to similar offerings.

Staging A temporary scaffolding used to support workers and materials; a slang term used to describe the process of preparing a home for viewing by prospective buyers.

Staking Identifying the boundaries of a parcel of land by placing stakes or pins in the ground, or by painting marks on stone walls or rocks. Staking shows the boundaries of the property but does not show the existence of possible encroachments.

Standard metropolitan statistical area A designation given to counties with at least one central city with 50,000 or more residents.

Standards of Practice The code of ethics created by the National Association of Realtors® describing the ethical behaviors licensees are expected to follow.

Standing loan A commitment by a construction lender to keep the money funded in the project in place for a specified period of time after the original period to allow the borrower time to secure permanent financing.

Starter A reference to an earlier title report on a particular piece of real property; a person's first residence or other real estate investment. A starter home, for example, is intended for first-time home buyers.

Starts The term used to indicate the number of residential units begun within a specific period of time.

State certified appraiser An appraiser certified by a state to conduct residential or general appraisals.

Statute A law established by an act of legislature.

Statute of frauds The part of a state law that requires certain instruments, such as deeds, real estate sales contracts, and certain leases, to be in writing to be legally enforceable.

Statute of limitations The law pertaining to the period of time within which certain actions must be brought to court.

Statutory lien A lien imposed on property by statute — a tax lien, for example — in contrast to an equitable lien, which arises out of common law.

Statutory right of redemption The right of a defaulted property owner to recover the property after its sale by paying the appropriate fees and charges.

Steering The illegal practice of channeling home seekers to particular areas to maintain the homogeneity of an area or to change the character of an area.

Step rate mortgage A loan which allows for a gradual interest rate increase during the first few years of the loan.

Step up lease A lease agreement which specifies certain increases in rent at certain intervals during the complete term of the lease. Also known as a graded lease.

Stepped up basis The income tax term used to describe a change in the adjusted tax basis of a property. The old tax basis is increased to reflect market value when a person inherits the property.

Stigmatized property A property that has acquired an undesirable reputation due to an event that occurred on or near it, such as violent crime, gang-related activity, illness, or personal tragedy. Some states restrict the disclosure of information about stigmatized properties.

Straight lease A lease agreement which specifies an amount of rent that should be paid regularly during the complete term of the lease. Also referred to as a flat lease.

Straight line depreciation A method of calculating depreciation for tax purposes, computed by dividing the adjusted basis of a property by the estimated number of years of remaining useful life.

Straight loan A loan in which only interest is paid during the term of the loan with the entire principal amount due with the final interest payment. Also known as a term loan.

Straight note A promissory note for a loan where payments of interest only are made at specific periods, with the principal balance due in one lump sum at the end of the loan term.

Straw man A person who purchases property that is then conveyed to another in order to conceal the identity of the eventual purchaser.

Street A fully improved roadway serving local traffic.

Strict liability A phrase meaning the owner is responsible to the injured party without excuse.

Strip center Any shopping area that is made up of a row of stores but is not large enough to be anchored by a grocery or department store; also known as a strip mall.

Structural alterations Changes to the supporting members of a building.

Structural defects Damage to the load-bearing portion of a home that affects the use of the home for dwelling purposes. Includes damage from shifting soil not due to earthquake or flood.

Structural density The ratio of the total ground floor area of a building to the total land area of the lot. The typical density for a general purpose industrial building is approximately 1 to 3.

Structure Any constructed improvement to a site; may include buildings, fences, garages, sheds, or utility buildings.

Studio An efficiency unit or apartment.

Sub agency The relationship under which a sales agent attempts to sell a property listed with another agent. Sub agency is common under multiple listing service arrangements.

Sub agreement of sale An agreement of sale between the original vendee of an agreement of sale and a new purchaser. The agreement creates no contractual relationship between the new purchaser (the sub vendee) and the owner of the property (the original vendor).

Sub lessee A person or business that holds the rights of use and occupancy under a lease contract with the original lessee, who still retains primary responsibility for the lease obligations.

Sub prime loan A loan offered to applicants with less than high credit ratings. Sub prime loans typically carry higher interest rates and higher fees.

Subagent One who is employed by a person already acting as an agent. Typically a reference to a salesperson licensed under a broker (agent) who is employed under the terms of a listing agreement.

Subcontractor A contractor who has been hired by the general contractor, often specializing in a certain required task for the construction project.

Sub-divider One who buys undeveloped land, divides it into smaller, usable lots, and sells the lots to potential users.

Subdivision A tract of land divided by the owner, known as the sub-divider, into blocks, building lots, and streets according to a recorded subdivision plat, which must comply with local ordinances and regulations; the most common type of housing development created by dividing a larger tract of land into individual lots for sale or lease.

Subdivision and development ordinances Municipal ordinances that establish requirements for subdivisions and development.

Subjacent support The support that the surface of the earth receives from its underlying strata.

Subject to Acquiring property with an existing mortgage, but not becoming personally liable for the debt.

Subject to clause Contingencies or special conditions for purchase and sale. Must be satisfied for the contract to become binding.

Subject to mortgage Situation where a buyer takes title to mortgaged real property but is not personally liable for the payment of the amount due. The buyer must make payments to keep the property; if he or she defaults, only the equity in the property is lost.

Subjective value The amount a specific person might pay to possess a property. Also referred to as personal value.

Sublease A lease from a lessee to another lessee. The new lessee becomes a sub lessee or tenant.

Subletting Leasing a premise by a lessee to a third party for part of the lessee's remaining term. Also known as subleasing.

Submittal notice Written notice by a broker to a seller with whom he or she has a listing agreement, stating the broker has shown the property and listing the prospect's name, address, and the selling price quoted.

Subordinate financing Any loan with a priority lower than loans that were obtained beforehand.

Subordinate loan A second or third mortgage obtained with the same property being used as collateral.

Subordinated classes Classes that have the lowest priority of receiving payments from underlying mortgage loans.

Subordination The act of sharing credit loss risk at varying rates among two or more classes of securities; relegation to a lesser position, usually in respect to a right or security.

Subordination agreement A written agreement between holders of liens on a property that changes the priority of mortgage, judgment, and other liens under certain circumstances.

Subordination clause A clause or document that permits a mortgage recorded at a later date to take priority over an existing mortgage.

Subpoena duces tecum A court order to produce books, records, and other documents.

Subrogation The substitution of one creditor for another, with the substituted person succeeding to the legal rights and claims of the original claimant. Subrogation is used by title insurers to acquire from the injured party rights to sue to recover any claims they have paid.

Subscribe To place a signature at the end of a document.

Subscription An agreement to buy a new securities issue.

Subsequent bona fide purchaser A person who purchases an interest in real property without actual or constructive notice or without any other superior rights in the property.

Subsequent rate adjustments The interest rate for ARMs that adjusts at regular intervals, sometimes differing from the duration period of the initial interest rate.

Subsequent rate cap The maximum amount the interest rate may increase at each regularly scheduled interest rate adjustment date on an ARM.

Subsidized housing Apartments, nursing homes, or single family dwellings that receive a government subsidy.

Subsidy A transfer of wealth intended to encourage specific behavior considered beneficial to the public welfare. The government may provide a rent subsidy, for example, to allow low income persons to obtain decent housing.

Substantial improvement Any improvement made to a building at least three years after the building was placed in service; improvements made over 25 percent of the value of the building over a two-year period.

Substitution An appraisal principle that states that the maximum value of a property tends to be set by the cost of purchasing an equally desirable and valuable substitute property, assuming that no costly delay is encountered in making the substitution.

Substitution of collateral A provision in a mortgage to allow the borrower to obtain a release of the original collateral by replacing it with another form of collateral satisfactory to the lender.

Sub-surface rights Ownership rights in a parcel of real estate to the water, minerals, gas, oil, and so forth that lie beneath the surface of the property.

Suit for possession A court suit initiated by a landlord to evict a tenant from leased premises after the tenant has breached one of the terms of the lease or has held possession of the property after the lease's expiration.

Suit to quiet title A court action intended to establish or settle the title to a particular property, especially when there is a cloud on the title.

Summary possession Eviction; the process used by a landlord to regain possession of the leased premises if the tenant has breached the lease or remains after the term of the lease.

Summons A legal notice that a lawsuit has been filed against a defendant, and that unless the defendant answers the complaint within a specified period of time, a default judgment will be entered against the defendant.

Super jumbo mortgage A term that classifies a loan that is over $650,000 for some lenders, and over $1,000,000 for others.

Superadequacy A component of real estate that is beyond what is needed in the structure. For example, a railroad spur in a residential neighborhood would be a superadequacy.

Superfund A commonly used name for the federal environmental cleanup law that requires previous owners to clean up waste on a particular site. Existence on the Superfund list imposes strict liability on the parties involved.

Supply The amount of goods available in the market to be sold at a given price. The term is often coupled with demand.

Supply and demand The appraisal principle that follows the interrelationship of the supply of and demand for real estate. As appraising is based on economic concepts, this principle recognizes that real property is subject to the influences of the marketplace just as is any other commodity.

Support deed A deed used to convey property that specifies that the buyer will support the grantor for the rest of his or her life. If proper support ceases, the courts will then disallow the deed.

Surcharge Additional rent charged to tenants who consume utility services in excess of the amounts allowed in the terms of the lease.

Surety A person who willingly binds himself to the debt or obligation of another party.

Surety bond An agreement by an insurance or bonding company to be responsible for certain possible defaults, debts, or obligations contracted for by an insured party; in essence, a policy insuring one's personal and/or financial integrity. In the real estate business a surety bond is generally used to ensure that a particular project will be completed at a certain date or that a contract will be performed as stated.

Surface rights Ownership rights in a parcel of real estate that are limited to the surface of the property and do not include the air above it (air rights) or the minerals below the surface (subsurface rights).

Surface water Diffused storm water, not a concentrated flow within a stream.

Surrender The cancellation of a lease by mutual consent of the lessor and the lessee.

Survey The process by which boundaries are measured and land areas are determined; the on-site measurement of lot lines, dimensions, and position of a house on a lot, including the determination of any existing encroachments or easements.

Survivorship The right of a joint tenant or joint tenants to maintain ownership rights following the death of another joint tenant.

Suspension A period of enforced inactivity.

Sweat equity A slang expression describing non-cash improvements that an owner adds to a piece of property. Refers to work performed personally by the owner or owners.

Sweetheart contract A slang expression describing a situation where a developer hires a subsidiary company to manage the developer's project.

Swing loan A short term loan that allows a homeowner to purchase a new home before selling the personal residence. Also called a bridge loan or a gap loan.

Syndicate A combination of people or firms formed to accomplish a business venture of mutual interest by pooling resources. In a real estate investment syndicate, the parties own and/or develop property, with the main profit generally arising from the sale of the property.

Synthetic lease A transaction that is considered to be a lease by accounting standards but a loan by tax standards.

Tacking Adding or combining successive periods of continuous occupation of real property by adverse possessors. This concept enables someone who has not been in possession for the entire statutory period to establish a claim of adverse possession.

Take off The estimate of materials needed to construct a building.

Takedown The time when a borrower actually accepts money from a lender under a line of credit or loan commitment.

Takeout financing A commitment to provide permanent financing following construction of a planned project. The takeout commitment is generally based on specific conditions, such as the completion of a certain number of units, or sales of a certain percentage of units. Most construction lenders require takeout financing.

Taking Similar to condemning, or any other interference with rights to private property, but a physical seizure or appropriation is not required.

Tangible personal property Property that can be seen, touched, and moved without great difficulty, excluding real estate.

Tangible property Real estate and other valuables that can be seen and touched.

Tax A charge levied on persons or things by a government.

Tax and lien search A title search issues to cover property registered in the Torrens system.

Tax base The determined value of all property that lies within the jurisdiction of the taxing authority.

Tax bracket The rate at which a taxpayer pays tax on income above a set amount. Tax rates are structured on a graduated basis, with rates increasing as income increases.

Tax certificate The document issued to a person as a receipt for paying delinquent taxes on a property owned by another, entitling the person to receive a deed to the property if the property is not redeemed within a certain period of time.

Tax credit An amount by which tax owed is reduced directly.

Tax deed An instrument, similar to a certificate of sale, given to a purchaser at a tax sale. See also certificate of sale.

Tax deferred exchange A transaction where a property is traded for the promise to provide a replacement like-kind property in the near future. By delaying the exchange, the party involved can defer taxable gains on the original property. Also known as a tax free exchange, or a 1031 exchange.

Tax lien A charge against property created by operation of law. Tax liens and assessments take priority over all other liens.

Tax map A document showing the location, dimensions, and other information pertaining to a parcel of land subject to property taxes. Usually kept as a public record at a local tax office or courthouse.

Tax participation clause A clause in a commercial lease that requires the tenant to pay a share of any increases in taxes or assessments above an established base year and amount.

Tax preference items Types of income or deductions that are added to adjusted gross income to calculate the alternative minimum tax (AMT).

Tax rate The ratio of a tax assessment to the amount being taxed. The tax rate is established according to assessed valuations.

Tax roll A record, that contains the descriptions of all land parcels (and their owners) located within the county.

Tax sale A court-ordered sale of real property to raise money to cover delinquent taxes.

Tax search The specific part of a title search that determines whether any unpaid taxes or special assessments create a lien against the property.

Tax service fee A fee that is charged for the purpose of setting up monitoring of the borrower's property tax payments by a third-party.

Tax shelter An investment that produces after-tax income that is greater than before-tax income. The investment shields income generated outside the investment itself.

Tax stop clause A clause in a lease that stops a lessor from paying property taxes above a certain amount.

Taxation The process by which a government or municipal public body raises monies to fund its operation.

Teaser rate A small, short-term interest rate offered on a mortgage in order to convince the potential borrower to apply.

Tenancy at sufferance Tenancy established when a person who had been a lawful tenant wrongfully remains in possession of property after the expiration of a lease.

Tenancy at will A license to use or occupy lands and buildings at the will of the owner. The tenant may leave the property at any time, or the owner may require the tenant to leave at any time.

Tenancy by the entirety The joint ownership, recognized in some states, of property acquired by husband and wife during marriage. Upon the death of one spouse the survivor becomes the owner of the property.

Tenancy for life A life estate; an interest in real or personal property that is limited in duration to the lifetime of its owner or some other designated person or persons.

Tenancy for years Tenancy created by a lease for a fixed term.

Tenancy in common A form of co-ownership by which each owner holds an undivided interest in real property as if he or she were sole owner. Each individual owner has the right to partition. Unlike joint tenants, tenants in common have right of inheritance.

Tenancy in partnership A form of co-ownership based on and regulated by a partnership agreement.

Tenancy in severalty Ownership of property by one person or one legal entity, like a corporation.

Tenant One who holds or possesses lands or tenements by any kind of right or title; called a lessee.

Tenant alternative costs The costs of remodeling or construction needed to make the premises usable by a particular tenant. Costs can be paid by the tenant, by the owner, or by both, depending on the agreement reached.

Tenant at will A person who possesses a piece of real estate with the owner's permission.

Tenant contributions All costs the tenant is responsible for in excess of normal rent payments. Cutting the grass, if required by the lease, is considered a tenant contribution.

Tenant improvement (TI) The upgrades or repairs that are made to the leased premises by or for a tenant.

Tenant Improvement allowance The specified amount of money that the landlord contributes toward tenant improvements.

Tenant mix The selection and location of retail tenants to maximize the income of the landlord and stimulate business in general.

Tenant union A local organization of local residential tenants working for their common interests and rights.

Tender An offer to perform an obligation; to perform under contract; to pay or deliver.

Tenement Possessions that are permanent and fixed; structures attached to land; older apartment units.

Tenure The nature of an occupant's ownership rights. Defines whether a person is an owner or a tenant.

Term The length that a loan lasts or is expected to last before it is repaid.

Termination of listing The cancellation of a broker employment contract.

Termite inspection An examination of a structure by a qualified person to determine the existence of termite infestation. Most sales contracts require a termite inspection.

Termite shield Metal sheeting placed in the exterior walls of a house near ground level to prevent termites from entering the house.

Testament A will.

Testate Having made and left a valid will.

Testator A person who has made a valid will. A woman often is referred to as a testatrix, although testator can be used for either gender.

Testimonium A clause that cites the act and date in a deed or other conveyance. A testimonium could read: "In witness whereof, the parties to these presents have hereunto set their hands and seals this day and year."

Thin capitalization An excessively high ratio of debt to equity in a corporation's capital structure.

Thin market A real estate market where there are few buyers and sellers and a slow rate of turnover of properties. Also called a limited market.

Third party A person who is not directly involved in a transaction or contract but may be involved or affected by it.

Third party origination A process in which another party is used by the lender to originate, process, underwrite, close, fund, or package the mortgages it expects to deliver to the secondary mortgage market.

Tidewater land Land beneath the ocean from the low tide mark to a state's outer territorial limits.

Tie in contract A contract in which one transaction depends on another.

Tier A strip of land six miles wide, extending east and west and numbered north and south according to its distance from the base line in the rectangular (government) survey system of legal description. Also referred to as a township strip.

Tight money market A situation where the supply of money is limited and the demand for money is high, resulting in high interest rates.

Time is of the essence A phrase in a contract that requires the performance of a certain act within a stated period of time.

Time price differential The difference between a property's purchase price and the higher price the same property would cost if purchased on an installment basis. (Finance charges would result in a higher cost.)

Time value of money An economic principle that states that the value of a dollar received today is worth more than the value of a dollar received in the future, since the dollar received in the future cannot be invested or enjoyed at present.

Time weighted average annual rate of return The regular yearly return over several years that would have the same return value as combining the actual annual returns for each year in the series.

Timeshare A form of ownership involving purchasing a specific period of time or percentage of interest in a vacation property.

Timeshare Ownership Plan (TSO) A form of timesharing in which a number of individuals hold title to a particular unit as tenants in common, entitling each to use the property at specified times during the year.

Tipping point A phrase referring to the point where sufficient numbers of minorities have moved into an area that results in large numbers of majority groups moving to another area.

Title The right to or ownership of land; the evidence of ownership of land.

Title company A business that determines that a property title is clear and that provides title insurance.

Title exam An analysis of the public records to confirm that the seller is the legal owner and there are no encumbrances on the property.

Title insurance A policy insuring the owner or mortgagee against loss by reason of defects in the title to a parcel of real estate, other than encumbrances, defects, and matters specifically excluded by the policy.

Title insurance binder A written promise from the title insurance company to insure the title to the property, based on the conditions and exclusions shown in the binder.

Title paramount A superior title.

Title report A preliminary report indicating the current state of the title. Does not describe the chain of title.

Title risk The potential impediments in transferring a title from one party to another.

Title search The process of analyzing all transactions existing in the public record to determine whether any title defects could interfere with the clear transfer of property ownership.

Title theory Some states interpret a mortgage to mean that the lender is the owner of mortgaged land. Upon full payment of the mortgage debt, the borrower becomes the landowner.

Tolling The suspension or interruption of the statute of limitations period.

Topography The nature of the surface of the land; the land's contour.

Topping off The highest point in a building's construction. In some cases a tree branch is attached to the topmost point in a project to signify the topping off point.

Torrens system A method of evidencing title by registration with the proper public authority, generally called the registrar, named for its founder, Sir Robert Torrens.

Tort A wrongful act that is neither a crime nor a breach of contract, but that still renders the perpetrator liable to the victim for damages. Trespassing is a tort.

Total Acres The complete amount of land area that is contained within a real estate investment.

Total assets The final amount of all gross investments, cash and equivalents, receivables, and other assets as they are presented on the balance sheet.

Total commitment The complete funding amount that is promised once all specified conditions have been met.

Total expense ratio The comparison of monthly debt obligations to gross monthly income.

Total inventory The total amount of square footage commanded by property within a geographical area.

Total lender fees Charges which the lender requires for obtaining the loan, aside from other fees associated with the transfer of a property.

Total loan amount The basic amount of the loan plus any additional financed closing costs.

Total monthly housing costs The amount that must be paid each month to cover principal, interest, property taxes, PMI, and/or either hazard insurance or homeowners' association dues.

Total of all payments The total cost of the loan after figuring the sum of all monthly interest payments.

Total principal balance The sum of all debt, including the original loan amount adjusted for subsequent payments and any unpaid items that may be included in the principal balance by the mortgage note or by law.

Total retail area The total floor area of a retail center that is currently leased or available for lease.

Total return The final amount of income and appreciation returns per quarter.

Townhouse An attached home that is not considered to be a condominium.

Township The principal unit of the rectangular (government) survey system. A township is a square with six-mile sides and an area of 36 square miles.

Township lines All the lines in a rectangular survey system that run east and west, parallel to the base line six miles apart.

Township tiers Township lines that form strips of land and are designated by consecutive numbers north or south of the base line.

Track record A developer or builder's reputation for producing on a timely and economical basis; the history of a real estate salesperson or broker's sales performance.

Tract A parcel of land generally held for subdividing; a subdivision.

Tract house A dwelling that has a similar style and floor plan to those of other houses in a development.

Tract index An index of records of title according to the description of the property conveyed, mortgaged, or otherwise encumbered or disposed of.

Trade fixture Any personal property that is attached to a structure and used in the business but is removable once the lease is terminated.

Trade in An agreement by a developer or broker to accept from a buyer a piece of real property as a part of the purchase price of another property.

Trade usage A uniform course of conduct followed in a particular trade, calling, or type of business.

Trading down The act of purchasing a property that is less expensive than the one currently owned.

Trading on the equity Agreeing to buy real estate and then assigning the purchase agreement to another buyer before closing takes place. Also known as "selling the paper."

Trading up The act of purchasing a property that is more expensive than the one currently owned.

Tranche A class of securities that may or may not be rated.

Trans Union Corporation One of the primary credit reporting bureaus.

Transactional broker Helps both the buyer and seller with paperwork and formalities in transferring ownership of real property, but is not an agent of either party.

Transfer of ownership Any process in which a property changes hands from one owner to another.

Transfer tax An amount specified by state or local authorities when ownership in a piece of property changes hands.

Tread The horizontal surface of a stair resting on the riser. The tread is the part of the stairs that is stepped on.

Treasury Index A measurement that is used to derive interest rate changes for ARMs.

Treble damages Damages provided for by statute in certain cases; calls for a tripling of the actual damages.

Trespass Unlawful entry or possession of property.

Trigger terms Specific credit terms, such as down payment, monthly payment, and amount of finance charge or term of loan.

Triple net lease A lease that requires the tenant to pay all property expenses on top of the rental payments.

Triplex A building with three apartment or townhouse units.

Truss A type of roof construction using a framework of beams or members that support the roof load and leaves wide spans between supports.

Trust Institution, called a trustee, to be held and administered on behalf of another person, called a beneficiary. The one who conveys the trust is called the trustor.

Trust account A separate bank account segregated from a broker's own funds, in which a broker is required to deposit all monies collected for clients. In some states is referred to as an escrow account.

Trust beneficiary The person for whom a trust is created.

Trust deed An instrument used to create a mortgage lien by which the borrower conveys title to a trustee, who holds it as security for the benefit of the note holder (the lender); also called a deed of trust.

Trust deed lien A lien on the property of a trustor that secures a deed of trust loan.

Trustee A fiduciary who oversees property or funds on behalf of another party; one who holds property in trust for another to secure performance of an obligation.

Trustee in bankruptcy A person appointed by the court to preserve and manage the assets of a party in bankruptcy.

Trustee's deed A deed executed by a trustee conveying land held in a trust.

Trustor A borrower in a deed of trust loan transaction.

Truth in lending The federal legislation requiring lenders to disclose the terms and conditions of a mortgage in writing

Tsunami damage Damage caused by tidal wave action.

Turn key project A project in which someone other than the owner is responsible for the construction of a building or for tenant improvements; a development in which the developer is responsible for completing the entire project on behalf of the buyer.

Turnover The rate at which tenants, salespersons, or employees leave; the frequency with which property in a particular area is bought and sold.

Two-step mortgage An ARM with two different interest rates: one for the loan's first five or seven years and another for the remainder of the loan term.

Two- to four-family property A structure that provides living space for two to four families while ownership is held in a single deed.

Ultra vires Acts of a corporation that are beyond its legal powers as set forth in its articles of incorporation.

Umbrella Partnership Real Estate Investment Trust (UPREIT) An organizational structure in which a REIT's assets are owned by a holding company for tax reasons.

Unbalanced improvement An improvement that is not in the highest and best use for the site. May either be an overimprovement or an underimprovement.

Unconscionability A legal doctrine whereby a court will refuse to enforce a contract that was grossly unfair or unscrupulous at the time it was made.

Under construction The time period that exists after a building's construction has started but before a certificate of occupancy has been presented.

Under contract The period of time during which a buyer's offer to purchase a property has been accepted, and the buyer is able to finalize financing arrangements without the concern of the seller making a deal with another buyer.

Underfloor ducts Floor channels that provide for the placement of telephone and electrical lines; allows for flexibility in use for commercial and office buildings.

Underground storage tank A tank below ground level that stores liquids, including fuels, industrial products, or waste.

Under improvement A structure or development of lower cost than the highest and best use of a site.

Underlying financing The first mortgage when a second mortgage is present.

Undersigned The person whose name appears signed at the end of a document; the subscriber.

Undertenant A person who holds property under a person who is already a tenant, such as in a sublease.

Underwriter A company, usually an investment banking firm, that is involved in a guarantee that an entire issue of stocks or bonds will be purchased.

Underwriters knot An approved knot according to code that may be tied at the end of an electrical cord to prevent the wires from being pulled away from their connection to each other or to electrical terminals.

Underwriting The process during which lenders analyze the risks a particular borrower presents and set appropriate conditions for the loan.

Underwriting fee A fee that mortgage lenders charge for verifying the information on the loan application and making a final decision on approving the loan.

Undisclosed agency A relationship between an agent and a client where the client is unaware that the agent represents the other party in the transaction. Many states require licensed agents to disclose their agency relationships.

Undivided interest An ownership right to use and possess a property that is shared among co-owners, with no co-owner having exclusive right to any portion of the property.

Undue influence Strong enough persuasion to overpower the free will of another and prevent him or her from making an intelligent and voluntary decision.

Unearned income Income derived from sources other than personal services. Rent is an example of an unearned income; wages are not.

Unearned increment An increase in the value of real estate unrelated to effort on the part of the owner—could be due to an increase in local property values, or example.

Unencumbered A term that refers to property free of liens or other encumbrances.

Unencumbered property Real estate with a free and clear title.

Unenforceable contract A contract that has all the elements of a valid contract, yet neither party can sue the other to force performance of it. For example, an unsigned contract is generally unenforceable.

Unethical Lacking in moral principles, failing to conform to an accepted code of behavior.

Unfair and deceptive practices A practice is unfair if it is immoral, unethical, or oppressive, or if it is intended to deceive or mislead.

Unfinished office space Space in a building without dividing walls, lighting, ceilings, air conditioning, and other services. Typically a landlord leases unfinished space after providing standard items or by providing a construction allowance amount to the tenant.

Uniform Building Code (UBC) A national code used mostly in the western states to regulate building standards.

Uniform Commercial Code (UCC) A codification of commercial law, adopted in most states, that attempts to make uniform all laws relating to commercial transactions, including chattel mortgages and bulk transfers. Security interests in chattels are created by an instrument known as a security agreement. To give notice of the security interest, a financing statement must be recorded. Article 6 of the code regulates bulk transfers — the sale of a business as a whole, including all fixtures, chattels, and merchandise.

Uniform Residential Appraisal Report (URAR) A standard form for reporting the appraisal of a dwelling. The URAR is required by major secondary mortgage purchases and includes checklists and definitions printed on the form.

Uniform Settlement Statement A special HUD form that itemizes all charges to be paid by a borrower and seller in connection with the settlement.

Uniformity An appraisal term used to describe assessed values that have the same relationship to market value, implying an equalization of the tax burden.

Unilateral contract A one-sided contract wherein one party makes a promise so as to induce a second party to do something. The second party is not legally bound to perform; however, if the second party does comply, the first party is obligated to keep the promise.

Unimproved land Land that has received no development, construction, or site preparation.

Unincorporated association An organization formed by a group of people. If the organization contains too many characteristics of a corporation, it may be treated as such for tax purposes.

Unit A suite of rooms making up a residence for one tenant. A unit generally has a separate entrance.

Unit in place method The appraisal method of estimating building costs by calculating costs of the physical components in the structure, with the cost of each item including its proper installation; also called the segregated cost method.

Unit value The value of an entire business entity, often used in the case of public utilities or railroads.

Unities The characteristics required to create a joint tenancy: unity of possession, time, possession, and title.

Universal agent A person empowered to do anything the principal could do personally.

Unjust enrichment When a person has received and retains money or goods that in fairness belong to another. A lawsuit is typically required to recover unjust enrichment.

Unlawful detainer A legal action that provides a method of evicting a tenant who is in default of a lease agreement; a summary proceeding intended to recover possession of a property.

Unmarketable title A title that contains substantial defects; may require a quiet title suit to repair.

Unrecorded deed A deed that transfers right of ownership from one owner to another without being officially documented.

Unsecured loan A loan that has no collateral or security pledged. An unsecured loan is approved based on the reputation and credit history of the borrower, not on the value of an underlying asset.

Up leg The replacement property purchased in a 1031 Exchange; so called because typically the taxpayer trades up in an exchange.

Upgrades Changes in design or improvements to a property after the purchase but before the closing date. The purchaser typically absorbs the cost for upgrades.

Upset date A date specified in a contract for when a building must be ready for occupancy, or when a buyer has the option of rescinding the agreement.

Upset price A minimum price set by the court in a judicial foreclosure. The property may not be sold below that price at public auction. The upset price typically does not exceed the fair market value of the property.

Upside down A slang phrase for a borrower owes more in debt for a property than the value of the property itself.

Upzoning Changing zoning classification from lower to higher use.

Urban Real estate located in an area of high density development; frequently refers to a city.

Urban renewal Redeveloping deteriorated sections of a city through demolition and new construction, or through extensive rehabilitation. Many urban renewal projects are government funded or subsidized.

Urban sprawl A term used to describe low density development in suburban areas adjacent to a major city. Residents of those areas typically commute back into the city for employment or shopping.

Usable square footage The total area that is included within the exterior walls of the tenant's space.

Use The particular purpose for which a property is intended to be employed.

Use tax Tax imposed on the purchaser or importer of tangible personal property.

Use value Subjective value of a special purpose property designed to fit the requirements of the owner but with little or no use to another owner.

Useful life The economic period during which a cash flow is expected; the period to depreciate a building for tax purposes.

Usufructuary right Interests that provide for the use of a property that belongs to another.

Usury Charging interest at a higher rate than the maximum rate established by state law.

Utilities Services like water, sewer, electricity, telephone, and gas that are generally required to operate a building or a residence. Also used to describe the charges for utility services.

Utility easement Use of another's property for the purpose of running electric, water, gas, or sewer lines.

Utility value The value in use to an owner, which includes the value of amenities attaching to the property.

VA loan A mortgage loan on approved property made to a qualified veteran by an authorized lender and guaranteed by the Department of Veterans Affairs to limit the lender's possible loss.

Vacancy factor The percentage of gross revenue that pro forma income statements expect to be lost due to vacancies.

Vacancy rate The percentage of space that is available to rent.

Vacant space Existing rental space that is presently being marketed for lease minus space that is available for sublease.

Vacate To move out.

Vacation home A dwelling used occasionally by the owner for recreational or resort purposes. Can be rented to others for a portion of the year.

Valid Having legally binding force. Legally sufficient and authorized by law.

Valid contract A contract that complies with all the essentials of a contract and is binding and enforceable on all parties.

Valuable consideration A type of promised payment upon which a promisee can enforce a claim against an unwilling promisor. Can be in the form of money or time.

Value The power of a good or service to command other goods in exchange for the present worth of future rights to its income or amenities; the worth of all the rights arising from ownership; the quantity of one thing that will be given in exchange for another.

Value added The anticipated increase in property value expected from fixing a condition causing depreciation or from improving a service or condition.

Variable payment plan Any mortgage repayment schedule that provides for periodic changes in the amount of monthly payments.

Variable rate Also called adjustable rate. The interest rate on a loan that varies over the term of the loan according to a predetermined index.

Variable Rate Mortgage (VRM) A loan in which the interest rate changes according to fluctuations in particular indexes.

Variance Permission obtained from zoning authorities to build a structure or conduct a use that is expressly prohibited by the current zoning laws; an exception from the zoning ordinances.

Vendee A buyer, usually under the terms of a land contract.

Vendor A seller, usually under the terms of a land contract.

Vendors lien A lien belonging to a vendor for unpaid purchase price of land, where the vendor has not taken any other lien or security beyond the personal obligation of the purchaser.

Veneer Wood or brick exterior that covers a less attractive or less expensive surface.

Vent A small opening to allow the passage of air.

Venture capital Unsecured money raised for high risk investments.

Venue The place where the cause of action arose, or the place where a jury is selected and a trial is brought.

Verification Sworn statements before a qualified officer that the contents of an instrument are correct.

Verification of Deposit (VOD) The confirmation statement a borrower's bank may be asked to sign to verify the borrower's account balances and history.

Verification of Employment (VOE) The confirmation statement a borrower's employer may be asked to sign in order to verify the borrower's position and salary.

Vested Having the right to draw on a portion or on all of a pension or other retirement fund.

Vested interest A right, interest, or title to real estate.

Vestibule A small entrance hall to a building or to a room.

Veterans Administration (VA) The federal government agency that assists veterans in purchasing a home without a down payment. In general a veteran who has served more than 120 days active duty is eligible for a home loan with no down payment.

Veto clause A clause in a shopping center lease that gives an anchor tenant the right to bar any lease between the landlord and another tenant. Designed to protect the business interests of the anchor tenant, veto clauses are typically invalid under antitrust regulations.

Vicarious liability The responsibility of one person for the acts of another.

Villa A one-story residence often owned as a condominium, and usually built in units of two or four, including an enclosed parking area and a yard.

Violation An act, deed, or condition contrary to law or to permissible use of real property.

Virtual storefront A retail business presence on the Internet.

Visual rights The right to prevent a structure like a billboard from being placed where it would obstruct a scenic view.

Voidable contract A contract that has no legal force or effect because it does not meet the essential elements of a contract.

Voluntary lien A lien placed on property with the knowledge and consent of the property owner.

Wainscoting Facing of the lower part of an interior wall.

Waiting period The period of time between initially filing a registration statement and the date it becomes effective.

Waiver The voluntary renunciation, abandonment, or surrender of a claim, right, or privilege.

Walk through Final inspection of a property just before closing to assure the buyer that the property is vacant and no damage has occurred.

Walkup An apartment building with several levels and no elevator.

Wall to wall carpeting Carpeting that fully covers the floor area in a room.

Warehouse A structure designed for the storage of commercial inventory.

Warehouse fee A closing cost fee that represents the lender's expense of temporarily holding a borrower's loan before it is sold on the secondary mortgage market.

Warehousing A term used to describe the packaging of a number of mortgage loans for sale in the secondary mortgage market.

Warranty A promise contained in a contract; a promise that certain stated facts are true.

Warranty deed A deed that contains a covenant that the grantor will protect the grantee against any and all claims.

Waste An improper use or an abuse of a property by a possessor who holds less than fee ownership, such as a tenant, life tenant, mortgagor, or vendee. Such waste ordinarily impairs the value of the land or the interest of the person holding the title or the reversionary rights.

Waste line A pipe that carries water from a bathtub, shower, sink, or other fixture, excluding a toilet.

Wasteland Land that is unfit for cultivation, or is unproductive, unimproved, or barren.

Wasting asset Something of value that deteriorates over time. An oil well is a wasting asset.

Water rights Common Law rights held by owners of land adjacent to rivers, lakes, or oceans, including restrictions on those rights and land ownership.

Water table The upper level at which underground water is normally found in a particular area.

Watercourse A running stream of water following a regular course or channel, usually possessing a bank and bed.

Waterfront property Real estate abutting a body of water like a lake, river, canal, or ocean.

Way A street, alley, or other thoroughfare permanently established for the passage of people or vehicles.

Wear and tear Physical deterioration of property as the result of use, weathering, and age.

Weep hole Small holes left in a wall to permit the drainage of surplus water.

Weighted average coupon The average, using the balance of each mortgage as the weighting factor, of the gross interest rates of the mortgages underlying a pool as of the date of issue.

Weighted average equity The part of the equation that is used to calculate investment-level income, appreciation, and total returns on a quarter-by-quarter basis.

Weighted average rental rates The average ratio of unequal rental rates across two or more buildings in a market.

Wet column A column containing plumbing lines.

Wetlands Land normally saturated with water. Marshes and swamps are wetlands. Wetlands are typically protected from development by environmental law.

Widows quarantine The period of time after a husband's death that a wife may remain in the house of her deceased husband without being charged rent.

Will A written document, properly witnessed, providing for the transfer of title to property owned by the deceased, called the testator.

Wipeout A decrease in property value caused by a public action (like a planning regulation) that creates negative results.

Withholding Holding back money designated for the payment of taxes.

Without recourse Words used in endorsing a note or bill to signify that the holder is not to seek recourse from the debtor in the event of nonpayment. The creditor only has recourse to the property.

Work letter A detailed addition to a lease defining all improvement work to be done by the landlord, and specifying what work the tenant will perform at his or her own expense.

Workers Compensation Acts Laws that require an employer to obtain insurance coverage to protect his or her employees who are injured in the course of their employment.

Working drawings The detailed blueprints for a construction project that comprise the contractual documents which describe the exact manner in which a project is to be built.

Workout The strategy in which a borrower negotiates with a lender to attempt to restructure the borrower's debt rather than go through the foreclosure proceedings.

Wraparound debt Mortgage debt in which the face amount of the loan overstates the actual debt; incorporates a special agreement between the parties for payment of debt service on the existing mortgage. The borrower pays the wraparound lender who in turn pays the debt service on the existing loan. The wrap is secured by a promissory note and mortgage document. The amount of the face value of the wrap is the sum of the outstanding balance on the existing mortgage plus the additional funds advanced to the borrower by the wraparound lender, with the result that the wrap "wraps around" the existing loan.

Wraparound loan Refinancing technique in which the new mortgage is placed in a secondary, or subordinate, position; the new mortgage includes both the unpaid principal balance of the first mortgage and whatever additional sums are advanced by the lender. In essence it is an additional mortgage in which another lender refinances the borrower by lending an amount over the existing first mortgage amount, but without disturbing the existence of the first mortgage. Wraparound loans are popular where the borrower wishes to obtain cash through the refinancing of an existing loan but the present lender is unwilling to do so at reasonable terms; and a conventional second mortgage from another lender may be unavailable or unworkable owing to excessively high interest and/or debt service; or the existing loan has an interest rate well below current market rates.

Wraparound mortgage A loan obtained by a buyer to use for the remaining balance on the seller's first mortgage, as well as an additional amount requested by the seller.

Writ of execution A court order authorizing an officer of the court to sell property of the defendant to satisfy a judgment.

Write down A procedure used in accounting when an asset's book value is adjusted downward to reflect current market value more accurately.

Write off A procedure used in accounting when an asset is determined to be uncollectible and is therefore considered to be a loss.

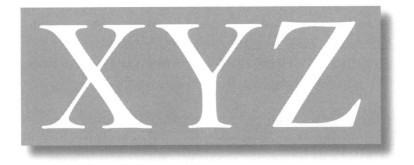

X A mark that can substitute for a signature in some cases, if a person cannot write. Requires the presence and affirmation of a notary.

X bracing Cross bracing in a partition.

Xylotomous The capacity of an organism to bore into wood. Termites, for example, have xylotomous capacity.

Yard The open grounds of a property.

Year to year tenancy A periodic tenancy in which the rent is reserved from year to year.

Yield The actual return on an investment, usually paid in dividends or interest.

Yield capitalization The lump-sum value of an income stream derived by using a discounted cash flow method. Used in the income appraisal approach.

Yield maintenance premium A penalty the borrower must pay to make investors whole in the event of early repayment of principal.

Yield spread The difference in income derived from a commercial mortgage and from a benchmark value.

Yield to Maturity (YTM) The internal rate of return on an investment. Evaluates all inflows and outflows of investment returns, and the timing of those occurrences.

Yuppie Slang term for young, upwardly mobile professionals, or for young singles or couples with high job skills and the potential for steady income increases.

Zero lot line A form of cluster housing development where individual dwelling units are placed on separately platted lots. Units may be attached to one another, but do not have to be.

Zone condemnation The demolition and clearance of entire areas to make room for new construction.

Zoning The act of dividing a city or town into particular areas and applying laws and regulations regarding the architectural design, structure, and intended uses of buildings within those areas.

Zoning estoppel The rule that bars the government from enforcing a new downzoning ordinance against a landowner who had incurred substantial costs in reliance on government assurances that he or she had met all zoning requirements before the new zoning took place.

Zoning ordinance The regulations and laws that control the use or improvement of land in a particular area or zone.

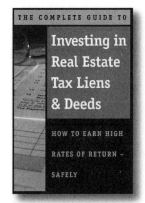

MORE GREAT TITLES FROM ATLANTIC PUBLISHING

THE PRE-FORECLOSURE REAL ESTATE HANDBOOK: INSIDER SECRETS TO LOCATING AND PURCHASING PRE-FORECLOSED PROPERTIES IN ANY MARKET

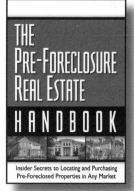

The Pre-Foreclosure Real Estate Handbook explains everything you need to know to locate and purchase real estate bargains from banks, public auctions, and other sources. Whether you are a first-time homeowner or an experienced property investor, *The Pre-Foreclosure Real Estate Handbook* is a tremendous guide for buying pre-foreclosed homes in any market. You will learn the simple formula (developed from real-life experience) that can build massive wealth through real estate foreclosures. This book is a resource for novices and pros alike; it will guide you through every step of the process including finding properties, negotiating, and closing on your first deal. Exhaustively researched, it will arm you with hundreds of innovative ideas that you can put to use right away. This book gives you the proven strategies, innovative ideas, and case studies from experts to help you get more with less time and effort.

346 Pages • Item # PFR-02 • $21.95

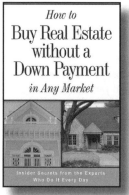

HOW TO BUY REAL ESTATE WITHOUT A DOWN PAYMENT IN ANY MARKET: INSIDER SECRETS FROM THE EXPERTS WHO DO IT EVERY DAY

This book explains everything you need to know to locate and purchase real estate with no down payment from individuals, banks, and other sources. Whether you are a first-time homeowner or an experienced property investor, this is a tremendous guide for buying real estate. You will learn the simple formula that can build wealth through real estate, with no money down. This proven formula works even if you have no real estate experience, bad or no credit, or very little money. This formula has been developed out of real-life experience. You will learn how to make smart real estate investments and use those investments to help you achieve financial success.

320 Pages • Item # BRN-02 • $21.95

FAST REAL ESTATE PROFITS IN ANY MARKET: THE ART OF FLIPPING PROPERTIES— INSIDER SECRETS FROM THE EXPERTS WHO DO IT EVERY DAY

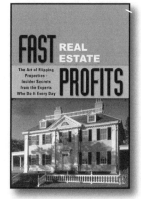

In real estate markets everywhere, real estate "flippers" have discovered that a small down payment, a little paint, some cleaning, and some time can net them tens (even hundreds) of thousands of dollars in profits, possibly tax-free. Finally there's a comprehensive, no-nonsense book that teaches you everything you need to build wealth through flipping properties quickly, legally, and ethically. You don't need great credit, a real estate license, or large sums of capital or experience to get started. There has never been a better time to invest in real estate. **288 Pages • Item # FRP-02 • $21.95**

To order call 1-800-814-1132 or visit www.atlantic-pub.com